P9-CND-302

DISCARDED

Cary Area Public Library
1606 Three Oaks Road
Cary, IL 60013

Advance Praise for *The Time Has Come*

"This book is a timely, incisive, and accessible wake-up call for men around the world. One of the things I'm asked most commonly in my work is: Where are the men discussing these issues? Why aren't more men taking up this cause? Where is the book that will speak to men about this topic? Well that book is here. It is vital reading for men everywhere, and I hope it will support a new wave of men and boys to become part of a battle that is as much theirs as it is women's." —LAURA BATES, author of *Everyday Sexism* and founder of the Everyday Sexism Project

"Kaufman provides a compelling case for men's stake in joining the fight for gender equity and for the benefits that we stand to gain in doing so. With humor, heart, and research he provides a relatable blueprint for men who want to embark on this important journey." —MATT McGORRY, actor (*Orange Is the New Black*, *How to Get Away with Murder*) and activist

"With a combination of compelling stories and facts, Michael Kaufman offers a timely and important case for engaging men in the ongoing fight for gender equality." —DEBORAH GILLIS, former president and CEO of Catalyst

"Being a male feminist isn't an option. It's a requirement, a duty, and a calling. This is not a book about history. This is a book about the future, and a guide on how to get there. We all owe a debt of gratitude to Michael Kaufman, not just for being the messenger, but for spending his life living the message." —ANDY DUNN, cofounder of Bonobos men's clothing stores

"This is a must-read book that will help us to rethink and redefine gender roles. It thoughtfully describes the deep-rooted stereotypes we need to challenge and the opportunities that will arise when we do. This is a book of hope." —ALINE SANTOS, Executive Vice President Global Marketing and Global Head of Diversity and Inclusion, Unilever

"One of the first men to stand up publicly against violence against women, Michael Kaufman has written a comprehensive and popular call to men to join the battle for gender equality not only through ending violence against women but also by supporting women's equality on an economic, social, political, and personal level. Give it to every man you know."
—JUDY REBICK, feminist, journalist, and author of *Heroes in My Head*

"Michael Kaufman makes a compelling case for why 'women's issues' are everyone's issues and for the role men play in challenging misogyny and creating more just societies." —SORAYA CHEMALY, writer and director of Women's Media Center Speech Project

"This is the global guidebook for all men, particularly our young men, to reflect and reconcile the global struggle and aspiration to redefine our lives as men. May all of us take what we learn from this book to action: listening to women and engaging men to work toward a better tomorrow for all."

—DAVID L. BELL, MD, MPH, medical director of The Young Men's Clinic at NewYork-Presbyterian Hospital/ Columbia University Medical Center

"Kaufman's *The Time Has Come* offers a personal and instructive appeal for men to take the journey from self-reflection to allyship to advocacy around gender equality." —WADE DAVIS, former NFL player, writer, and educator

"Michael Kaufman forces us to face the central question in working to stop violence against women and for gender equality: if not now, when?" —OLIVIA CHOW, distinguished visiting professor at Ryerson University, former member of the Parliament of Canada, and survivor of physical and sexual violence

"Just as I expected, a thought-provoking book from Michael Kaufman. He is so right that the time has truly come for men to step it up for a gender equal world, to listen to the voices of women—and to take joint action. Gender equality is not a woman's problem; it is a societal issue, an economic issue, and an imperative for driving progress for all." —KATJA IVERSEN, president and CEO of Women Deliver

"From a long career at the forefront of the movement for gender justice, Michael Kaufman offers a beautifully written, compelling vision for how men's lives can improve—indeed, are already improving—as sexism and its supporting structures give way. He models both compassion and an uncompromising commitment to truth as he traces new possibilities for men and paints an enticing picture of what lies just ahead. Parents of boys will find Kaufman's message essential and encouraging."

—MICHAEL C. REICHERT, author of *How to Raise a Boy: The Power of Connection to Build Good Men*

"While progress toward achieving gender equity in media and entertainment is still glacial in many areas, we need to engage men and boys to stand by our sides, to help give us a stronger voice, get us a seat at the table, and be our champions in order to make systemic change. Michael Kaufman's book is a must-read!"

—MADELINE DI NONNO, CEO of the Geena Davis Institute on Gender in Media

"*The Time Has Come* is world-changing and life-changing for women and for the men who make a stand."   —GARY BARKER, founder and CEO of Promundo, Washington, D.C., and member of the UN Secretary-General's Network of Men Leaders

ALSO BY MICHAEL KAUFMAN

Cracking the Armour: Power, Pain, and the Lives of Men

AS EDITOR

Beyond Patriarchy:
Essays by Men on Pleasure, Power, and Change

Community Power and Grassroots Democracy:
The Transformation of Social Life
with Haroldo Dilla Alfonso

Theorizing Masculinities
with Harry Brod

FICTION

The Possibility of Dreaming on a Night Without Stars

The Afghan Vampires Book Club
with Gary Barker

DISCARDED

THE TIME HAS COME

Why Men Must Join the Gender Equality Revolution

MICHAEL KAUFMAN

Cary Area Public Library
1606 Three Oaks Road
Cary, IL 60013

COUNTERPOINT
Berkeley, California

To Nathan, Liam, and Nathan—
my father, my son, my grandson—with all my love

The Time Has Come

Copyright © 2019 by Michael Kaufman
First hardcover edition: 2019

All rights reserved under International and Pan American Copyright
Conventions. No part of this book may be used or reproduced in any manner
whatsoever without written permission from the publisher, except in the case
of brief quotations embodied in critical articles and reviews.

ISBN: 978-1-64009-119-1

The Library of Congress Cataloging-in-Publication Data is available.

Jacket design by Sarah Brody
Book design by Jordan Koluch

COUNTERPOINT
2560 Ninth Street, Suite 318
Berkeley, CA 94710
www.counterpointpress.com

Printed in the United States of America
Distributed by Publishers Group West

10 9 8 7 6 5 4 3 2 1

Contents

The Time Has Come

1

THE TIME
HAS COME

The public world of gender relations is exploding around us. The private world of relationships, families, and sex is a minefield of power and love. There has never, ever, in the eight-thousand-year history of our male-dominated world, been a moment quite like this. You and I are living it. The gender equality revolution.

It's in our offices and factories in the quest for equal pay, for women's advancement, and against sexual harassment. It's on college campuses, in downtown neighborhoods, and suburban homes in the fight to end violence against women. It's the struggle by parents to redefine whose work it is to raise children and for society to provide the resources for parents to do the job well. It's the back-and-forth skirmishes to ensure that women have the unalienable right to physical autonomy, including choosing whether or not to become a parent. It's a powerful rethinking of how we raise girls and boys. It's a celebration of the right to love who we want to love and define who we want to be. It's a push for more, and more diverse, women in politics and in the boardroom.

The gender equality revolution is coming on fast and coming on strong.

It's time for men to join the fight for gender equality.

Fifty years of feminist organizing came to a head in early 2017. Millions of women and hundreds of thousands of men greeted the election of Donald Trump with some of the largest demonstrations the United States has ever seen. People joined in around the world. They were not only reacting to Trump's boast of assaulting women but also were there to celebrate the impact of feminism and to show they would resist any attempts to roll back progress on women's rights.

The people in the streets and the tens of millions more who cheered in support inserted new life into decades of feminism and powered everything that was to come. Within months, revelations of sexual harassment and assault poured out of Silicon Valley; the film, theater, and TV industries; and the corporate world at home and abroad. The betrayal of trust, abuse of authority, and the denigration of women by men in positions of power pounded into our brains. As #MeToo and #TimesUp captured our attention, discussions quickly moved from newsrooms to dining rooms, staff rooms, and locker rooms. Men asked wives, daughters, and coworkers: *Did anything like that ever happen to you?* and a frightening number of women answered, *Yes, of course, but why has it taken men so long to listen?*

The spreading shock waves are giving new impetus to demands in our workplaces for equal pay and equal access to all jobs. The millennia-long affirmative action program for my half of the species simply can't go on. The shock waves are bringing new energy to concerns about the panoply of violence—verbal, sexual, emotional, physical—that countless women still experience. They are bringing more attention to the critical need for quality, affordable childcare and for parental leave.

And for men? More and more of us are realizing we cannot stay silent. We know we must speak out and we must examine our own attitudes and behaviors. But we're also realizing that it's time to rethink and reshape what it means to be a man because of the destructive *and* self-destructive ways we've defined manhood.

When I Chose to Join the Fight

For almost four decades, the focus of my work as an educator, advisor, speaker, activist, and writer has been on engaging men to promote gender equality and to explore how gender equality is bringing positive changes to men's lives.

I grew up in the 1950s and 1960s in a pretty traditional North American home (first in Ohio, then North Carolina, then in Ontario, Canada). Dad was a doctor, Mom a housewife. But equality was assumed. There was never a question whether my four sisters would go to university (still not the norm at that time) and pursue professional lives. We all knew that Mom was in charge of household finances and was the better driver to boot.

I began university in 1969 in that most exciting era when every moment seemed to bring fresh possibilities for change and we knew our generation was remaking the world. And despite our inexperience and naïveté, it was true: the civil rights movement in the United States, the antiwar and student movements around the world, the great cultural upheavals in music and relationships, then the women's movement and the beginning of the gay rights and environmental movements have, indeed, changed the world.

All my women friends and girlfriends were feminists. I supported women's rights. Around 1971 or '72, I wrote my first essay on men and feminism.

And yet, on some level, I didn't really think feminism and gender equality, or what we then called women's liberation, should be central to my life. Sure, I knew there were sexist things I shouldn't say and causes I should support. But no one, women or men, was expecting much active involvement from men. I didn't spend much time examining my life as a man, or the invisible privileges I enjoyed, especially as a middle-class straight man who happened to have white skin. Nor did I think much about the price I paid for trying to fit into the rigid ideals of manhood.

Then in 1979, while I was working on my PhD in political science, I was in upstate New York doing a weeklong training program to be a peer counselor. Organizers announced that the men (we were a minority) would start each morning with a men's group. Kind of weird, I thought, but here I was.

When I arrived for the group on the first morning, I looked at the five or so other guys and instantly realized I had nothing in common with them. I pegged them right away: that one was a jock, that one a stockbroker, and so on. What bothered me wasn't their jobs, but the fact that they all seemed very successful in the game of Being A Man. Me, on the other hand? In spite of whatever boxes I'd ticked—school, girlfriends, pick-up sports, car, education—I never felt I really lived up to the expectations of manhood. You know, never tough enough, plus I had all sorts of vulnerabilities that were inconsistent with an armor-plated masculinity. I figured I was the only guy who felt that way.

We introduced ourselves. I did have people's jobs more or less pegged. But as each man spoke, we all said the exact same thing: no matter how successful we were, no matter how things looked on the outside, we never felt like a "real man."

Turned out, to my great surprise, I wasn't the only guy who felt that way.

Back in Toronto, within a few years—in the midst of an exciting time as a new father trying to equally share the parenting jobs with Maureen, my partner in those years, writing my PhD dissertation, and teaching university—I volunteered to lead a group for men to explore our lives as men. I noticed there was virtually nothing written about men and masculinity from a pro-feminist position, so once

I finished my PhD thesis, I started research that led to one of the first books in the field, *Beyond Patriarchy: Essays by Men on Pleasure, Power, and Change.*[1] By the late 1980s, I was doing occasional talks in schools and at a handful of professional or business conferences. I got involved in some tiny pro-feminist men's networks in the United States, Canada, and Europe.

Next fork in the road. 1989. A hot summer night. At an outdoor Pete Seeger and Arlo Guthrie concert, I ran into my friend Gord Cleveland and we got to talking about a case in the news. A man (and, as it later turned out, a serial abuser of women) in Quebec was trying to prevent his ex-girlfriend from obtaining an abortion. There, right after the concert, inspired by the civil rights, worker's rights, and antiwar songs, we decided it was high time that men, as men, spoke out in support of women's right to have an abortion.

We started a one-shot effort called Men for Women's Choice. We wrote a short statement and then did something that no one had done before: we approached well-known men from across the social, political, and religious spectrum and asked them to sign the statement that appeared as a large ad in the country's most prominent newspaper.

And that seemed to be it, until two years later. In early September 1991, two men, Jack Layton and Ron Sluser, wanted to speak out as men appalled by men's violence against women and approached me.

Two years earlier, fourteen women university students had been murdered in Montreal by a man enraged by feminism and the gains women were making. Mass murders are unusual in Canada and this horrible act galvanized the country. Although many individuals expressed their horror, and I did a few interviews in the national media, we men dropped the ball in coming up with any sort of concerted response. Then, in the summer of 1991, Jack's and Ron's partners challenged them to do something and phoned me.[2] Remembering Men for Women's Choice, they suggested we write a statement and approach a diverse group of prominent men to sign on.

I felt, however, that we needed more than a small number of well-meaning men to speak out. I proposed combining a founding statement with some sort of activity leading up to December 6, the second anniversary of the so-called Montreal Massacre, perhaps involving men wearing or displaying various things in white, from white flowers to white arm bands to white ribbons.

At the time, ribbon symbols were virtually unknown. Ten years earlier, some people in the United States tied large yellow ribbons around trees in support of US hostages in Iran. The red AIDS ribbon was created the same year we started White Ribbon, but it had yet to achieve its public presence.

I suggested the color white for several reasons. One was symbolic. White is a color associated in Western cultures with peace: the flag of peace, the peace dove. In some Asian countries, it is a color associated with death and mourning. We wanted a color that men would feel comfortable wearing—a more limited palette at the time. And it was also very practical: many men wouldn't have a clue where to buy ribbon, but I figured anyone could tear up an old T-shirt or sheet.

Things stalled. Jack was running for mayor, which occupied all his time; my father had heart surgery and I briefly left the city. Nothing much happened until an annual men's conference in October where I presented the idea. Men from Ottawa, London, Kingston, Montreal, and Toronto responded enthusiastically.

I wrote a founding statement. Ron and I tracked down phone numbers for prominent men in the arts, sports, politics, religion, business, and the labor movement and we faxed and phoned whomever we could find. Meanwhile, groups in other cities were garnering local support.

When we launched the campaign a month later, so unusual was this (and so great had been the impact of women's organizing and the untapped concern of men) that our effort made front pages across the country. Literally overnight, men were fashioning white ribbons. We estimated that one hundred thousand men took part.

The campaign spread to Norway and Sweden in the early 1990s. It has since spread to about ninety countries. In some, there is a permanent White Ribbon organization (national but sometimes local or statewide, as in the case of Massachusetts). In some, it has come and gone (and sometimes come back again). In many places, it is an annual campaign organized by an NGO, company, student union, or United Nations or government body; in some it's become a symbol associated with speaking out against violence against women with no particular organization attached.

In a few cases, the campaign is a very prominent national effort. For example, the annual White Ribbon Day in Australia has events all over the country: in schools, the police and armed forces, government buildings, workplaces, and community centers. More importantly, it works year-round, including a program based in schools. Its Workplace Accreditation Program helps companies develop policies and practices not only to prevent sexual harassment in the workplace, but also to support workers experiencing domestic violence.

The campaign in rural Cambodia has seen convoys of ox-drawn carts moving along dirt roads. Former gang members in New Zealand conduct an annual motorcycle ride across the country to speak to men in communities big and small. Nelson Mandela led a march in South Africa where men and women wore white ribbons. Parliamentarians in Europe have spoken out. Students on US college campuses have organized classroom events. The Pakistani campaign has trained journalists in how to responsibly report issues around this violence, pushed religious authorities to raise their voices, and even organized a White Ribbon wrestling tournament in one rural community. The Chinese campaign runs a year-round hotline staffed by trained volunteers. In Brazil, the campaign pushed for and won a national day focused on the eradication of violence against women.

I never had a paid job with White Ribbon, although during the '90s it was sometimes half-time volunteer work until I pulled out of active participation in the early 2000s, realizing it was time for others to step forward.

With White Ribbon we did something that no one in the

world had done before: we figured that millions and millions of men should and would speak out on something that, until then, had been defined both incorrectly and condescendingly as "only" a women's issue.

We also believed we needed to reach out to men across the social and political spectrum. We were not looking for broad agreement on all social or political issues, or even on all the issues that were part of the women's movement. We focused on working alongside women to help end the violence that too many women and girls were experiencing.

We knew that the majority of men didn't use violence in our relationships. But we knew we'd been silent about the violence and, through that silence, had allowed the violence to continue.

We were the first mass effort anywhere in the world working to directly and broadly engage men in supporting women's rights that positively challenged men to examine our own attitudes and behavior and to speak out *as men*.

This is the same approach I have applied to all my work, whether it's to promote workplace equality or more active and involved fatherhood, or supporting women's reproductive rights. And, due to the hard work of so many remarkable men and women, this is now the mainstream approach around the world for engaging men to support women's rights: Approach men as allies. Reach out to men with positive messages of change. Challenge our fellow men but carry the banner of empathy and compassion. Understand the paradox of men's strange and often painful experiences within male-dominated societies. Encourage men to honestly examine our own privileges and mistakes, but don't assume collective guilt or blame. Develop broad public partnerships on a range of issues, working alongside those you may disagree with on other things. In particular, work in partnership with women and women's organizations, listen to women's diverse voices, learn from the leadership and strength of women. Understand the capacity of men for change; understand the capacity of men for decency and love.

A year after cofounding White Ribbon, I left the academic world to write books and hopefully make a useful contribution as a speaker, advisor, and trainer focused on engaging men to promote gender equality and end violence against women. That work takes me across the continent and around the world where, over and over, I meet inspiring women and men.

Like so many others, I continue to be struck by how absolutely personal the great issues of feminism are (as captured in the feminist maxim "the personal is political"). I would get so angry when my wife, Betty, experienced sexism and racism in her job as the lead architect doing large, institutional projects. As I watched my stepdaughter Chloé develop as a writer in Hollywood, not only was I horrified about predatory men in her business but I also questioned whether men in positions of power were ready to support women's voices and women's careers. And I grew angry as I watched my son Liam during his first year as a father wrestling with his immediate boss at the time, the president of a software company, who had little conception that two-income families put new demands not only on women, but on men as well. However personal, though, ultimately my activism was about the countless women I would never know—even if I somehow had no personal connection to these issues (although of course we all do), I'd still be doing my best to support gender equality.

My actions, while personal, are also about the boys and men who are struggling to redefine their lives as men. A few years ago I was at the United Nations in New York for the launch of a report I coauthored. *The State of the World's Fathers* charts the incredible transformation in the role of fathers taking place right now around the world. It's a transformation with profound implications for our families, for advancing gender equality, for women's career opportunities, for children's well-being, for men's priorities, and for the organization of work life. Several leaders from UN agencies, NGOs, and the private sector spoke about how we have clear evidence of worldwide changes in the role of fathers that are putting men foursquare onto the gender equality agenda. But, I added, for these changes to really move forward, we need a combination of individual change within families and big and bold policy initiatives. Individual action and broad social change, individual education and new laws, personal commitment and a dramatic shift in social values and priorities. It's all part of the gender equality revolution.

Over the past three decades, a handful of others and I have pushed to see our approach to engage men move from the margins into the mainstream. Back in the 1980s I knew the names of many of the pro-feminist male scholars, educators, and activists in much of the world. It's not that my Rolodex was so impressive; it's simply that there were pitifully few of us. And throughout the '90s and into the noughts, the idea of mainstream approaches to bringing men into the fight for women's rights and for profound changes in the lives of men was seen by many women's organizations as a waste of time, a waste of money, a deception, or a distraction.

And yet, small numbers of remarkable feminist men and feminist women focusing on men's lives plugged away around the world—scholars and researchers, activists and educators, policy makers and campaigners. I continue to learn so much from them. Men and women started new research or activist organizations, or departments within existing organizations, focused on men. Women who my male colleagues and I admired continued to challenge us to do more and do it better.

Meanwhile, feminists were meeting with successes but still faced powerful men and male-dominated institutions that blocked their efforts. But hard work and new organizations combined with the dictates of reality to produce a different approach to men's place within the gender equality revolution. Most women's rights organizations and so many women working as policy makers or as corporate leaders now feel it is critical to find ways to engage men in struggles for women's rights. Organizations such as UN Women, the UN Population Fund, Oxfam, and so many others now have programs and initiatives to work with men and boys; they know we must change how we raise boys to be men. Lest I be misunderstood, no woman thinks that men should be riding to their rescue. No organization wants to compromise women's leadership and independent women's action. No organization thinks they should spend less on programs and services for women and girls—and in fact are vigilant, as we all must be, that efforts to engage men don't take scarce funding or resources away from women.

I write not only in the context of growing interest in involving men to end violence against women and support women's rights. I write at a pivotal moment when these struggles are riveting our attention in companies and sports leagues, schools and homes. And when we are finally reaching the highest levels of government discussion and decision making.

I looked around the table at the presidents of France and the United States, the chancellor of Germany, the prime ministers of the United Kingdom, Italy, Japan, and Canada. It was the summer of 2018 and I was at the G7 table for a discussion about gender equality.

I was there as a member of the G7 Gender Equality Advisory Council established by Canadian prime minister Justin Trudeau. It was a wonderful council, cochaired by Melinda Gates and Isabelle Hudon and involving an amazing group of women leaders including Phumzile Mlambo-Ngcuka, Executive Director of UN Women and Under-Secretary-General of the United Nations; Nobel Peace Prize winner Malala Yousafzai; Winnie Byanyima, executive director of Oxfam International; Katja Iversen, president of Women Deliver; and sixteen other professors, activists, army generals, policymakers, educators, former presidents, and community and Indigenous leaders. I was the only male in the group and I was honored to be in the presence of each and every one of them.[3]

Trudeau wanted to do something that no one had ever done before: make gender equality central to all the discussions of the G7; not only at the actual summit but also at the yearlong round of ministerial meetings and consultations. It was a first for both the G7 and, as far as I can make out, any of these various international gatherings—G7, G8, G20, APEC, and many others. Trudeau was matching the discussion with actions by his government: a cabinet that was half women, gender equality articulated into foreign policy, a national budget process that used gender-based analysis in all areas of government expenditure and programming, and changes in parental leave to increase fathers' participation.

Our Gender Equality Advisory Council had already worked extremely hard in the preceding months, volunteers that we were. We'd been writing reports and responding to G7 preparatory documents, and some of us had taken part in ministerial meetings where we brought a gender lens to discussions of national security, jobs and the future of work, international development, and climate change.

And now, there we were. We met with the leaders of the G7 countries for an hour—presenting an ambitious agenda for action—and then they discussed these issues on their own for another hour.

Yes, it was a strange moment. The heights of political power. The deafening sound of cameras clicking before photographers and reporters were ushered out the door.

The phalanxes of Secret Service, plainclothes Royal Canadian Mounted Police, and who knows who jamming the corridors outside the meeting room. And yet, it was also utterly mundane, just another meeting at another table: people occasionally shared a quick aside with a neighbor, a few leaders fiddled with their translation devices to find the right channel, and one fidgeted and seemed rather out of place.

Whatever the problems with these types of meetings (including their staggering security budgets) and whatever criticism I might have about some of the policies of these leaders, it was an incredible moment. It shows the world-shaking impact of feminism. It led to at least one bit of concrete action: countries pledged $3.8 billion for girls' education in the Global South—the United States was the only country that didn't put up a penny. In a wide range of discussions during the course of the year, government ministers and policy makers were addressing women's rights, the impact of policies on women and girls, and the role of men and the lives of men and boys.

From dining rooms to the halls of power, gender equality is definitely on the table.

This book is all about how men can join women—in part by women reaching out to men and challenging us, and in part by men reaching out to our brothers—in continuing what is the greatest revolution in human history: the work to win women's rights, gender justice, and gender equality.

And as we shall see, winning those rights and the massive changes of our era that started as a women's revolution are already bringing enormous benefits to men and to the world.

What that means, and what I aim to show you, is that feminism is the greatest gift that men have ever received.

However, it does not come for free. It means challenging inequality and also challenging oneself. It often requires challenging the beliefs and actions of other men around us. It means listening to the voices of women and daring to look at forms of power and privilege we have enjoyed as men that might have been invisible to us. Yet I am absolutely certain that men's commitment to a gender-equitable future will transform men's lives in positive ways.

Men's embrace of this change has certainly been sparked and encouraged by women. But ultimately we need to find effective ways to bring in men as active proponents of change. This starts with men being part of the struggle for women's rights. In that, we can take some inspiration from two men living half a world apart.

Two Men

We often think of leadership as what takes place at the apex of a company, a government, or a team. But leadership is also about our actions in our neighborhoods, over a glass of beer, or in our homes. Sometimes it's a small gesture, while other times it's far more dramatic. And while we need new government policies, changes in laws and action at the highest levels, some of the most effective change happens in our communities or at a kitchen counter.

This includes men taking leadership alongside women to work for the right for women to live free of violence. After all, this right is not only critical for women's safety, health, and emotional well-being, it is a precondition for women's equal participation in the work force, education, and politics. It's also the precondition for future generations of girls *and* boys to grow up in loving and secure homes, free of the emotionally and intellectually debilitating impact of violence on children.

I met a man from the Swat Valley, a remote, mountainous region of Pakistan. He was young, but already his face was gaunt and angular, as if blowing sand had chiseled rock fractured by cold winter nights. His hair was thick and dark, and by the end of the afternoon, dense stubble had formed on his face. When I first sat down with him in a small restaurant, his shoulders were slumped and he glanced around with caution, perhaps even suspicion. But when we talked, a fierce passion came into his eyes and his soft voice rose when he spoke of the day he graduated from law school and returned home to Swat. (At the time, many years ago, I hadn't heard of this region; now I know it is where Malala and her family are from.)

While he was away at law school, the generals in power, in an attempt to appease the rising number of Islamic fundamentalists, were making use of something called the Hudood Ordinances. It was a reactionary interpretation of Islamic law that proclaimed, among other things, that if a girl or woman made an accusation of rape, she had to produce four male witnesses to substantiate the crime. As you might imagine, no woman was ever able to meet this requirement. Not only would their accusations then be branded as false, but these women could then be charged with adultery. If found guilty, they could be put in prison; they could be put to death.

This man saw all this and said to himself, *This is against the legal tradition of Pakistan.* And he thought, *This is not what I believe are the teachings of Islam.* He decided to defend these women and he quickly found success, if not in leading to charges against the men who had committed sexual assault, at least in receiving acquittals of adultery for these girls and women.

The response of the powers that be was to throw him into prison. When he told me this, I instantly imagined the hardship and suffering he underwent in this prison in a remote region of Pakistan. And then I imagined even worse: how the other male prisoners had tormented him when they discovered why he was there.

Whatever I imagined, however, was wrong. When the other male prisoners found out he was in prison for defending women in their community, they went on a hunger strike. It was a place where food was never plentiful, but they refused to eat even what little they had until this man was released. It did not take long, for within days, the rusty door was unlocked and he walked away free.

Another story, from half a world away: It was a number of years ago. I was in a small town on the shore of Lake Huron helping folks on a local campaign to promote equality and end violence against women. The air was crisp that night in early winter, and already there was a layer of powdery snow on the ground. Christmas lights glowed on lampposts as I drove toward a church to talk about the problem of violence against women. I spoke that night about the epidemic of this violence, from the most commonplace sexual harassment at work to the most horrific moments of murder; of the pioneering, difficult, and often heroic work of women around the world; and of the White Ribbon Campaign.

After my talk, a man approached me. I noticed his hesitation to speak. I was pretty tired and steeled myself for what I imagined would be a long, impromptu counseling session. Patiently, he waited until other people had asked me a question or exchanged a few words. He didn't speak until everyone had left.

Finally, with eyes unable to meet mine and in a quiet voice, he asked me: "Is it okay if, well, you know, if people make copies of White Ribbon things?" I assumed he meant making copies of our posters and flyers, or our materials for distribution in schools or workplaces.

"Of course," I said. "We encourage you to take whatever we do and adapt it for your own use." Still wary, he asked, "Even your TV ad?" At the time we had a thirty-second television message about the importance of men speaking out. "That too," I said. He still didn't look at me. Finally he said, "Is it okay to make more than one copy?" I said he could make all the copies he wanted.

Only then did he relax and look at me.

He said, "Well, I've made dozens and dozens of copies."

He owned a small shop that repaired electronic equipment, especially VCRs. He had made many copies of our TV message and whenever he repaired a VCR, he slipped in the videocassette and returned it to the owner without saying a word. So when his customers switched on their TVs to see if the VCR worked, suddenly they would see a message about speaking out against men's violence toward women.

It's a long way from a small town in North America to a bustling city in the Swat region of Pakistan. One of these men risked much more than the other. But these two men represent the millions of men and boys around the world who, right now, are speaking out to their friends at school or work, or who are raising their sons with a strong belief in the equal rights of women. There are millions of men who are supporting campaigns big and small, who are taking initiatives to make their own lives, workplaces, and homes more gender equitable.

There are so many of us, so many men, who are now realizing these changes stand to make our own lives better too.

There are so many men who realize the time has come.

2

LISTENING TO THE VOICES OF WOMEN

K athy is thirty-six. When her twins were born, she took two years away from her job at a consulting firm. When she returned to work, something changed. Before her pregnancy, she'd clearly been on track to become a partner. Partners would invite her to lunch. She'd be asked for her opinion in a way that she knew was testing her for bigger things. There was open talk about her future. And now? It is clear she has entered a different bracket. Good worker. Smart as a whip. Creative. Gets the job done ... But just not partner material.[1]

Maria has a summer job. Her boss has a local reputation as being an outstanding man and a family guy. Two weeks in, she drives with him to a meeting. "Learn some of the ropes around here," he says. She's grateful. After the meeting, they return to the car. Instead of starting it, he turns to her and asks if she enjoyed the meeting. She says it was interesting. He leans fractionally closer and says, "Now that you're with us the whole summer, what do you say you and I get to know each other a bit better?"

Jeanette notices something. She is at a department meeting in her plant. She makes what she thinks is a pretty good point. There are a few nods, but the idea doesn't get picked up. That is until one of the men makes the exact same point five minutes later and from that moment on it is "Don's idea." That night she tells her boyfriend. He tries to console her. "It's probably just the way the meeting flowed. Don't let it get you down." But it keeps bugging her. She remembers another meeting when one of the other women made a suggestion. Everyone was lukewarm about it until one of the men said it was a good idea and, only then, was it taken seriously.

Aisha is in her first job in the kitchen of a very cool restaurant. Great food. Very hip chef. She's not there more than an hour before he unloads on her, not just barking out the orders but telling her how useless she is. Later, he says, "You may be hot, but if you don't move quicker, that main's gonna be stone cold." Later, his hand rests so long on her back she starts to feel uncomfortable. She talks to a girlfriend who says, "Yeah, well that's the restaurant business. Guys get yelled at too." She keeps her eyes open for this. It's true. It's a hierarchical setup. Chef is boss/father/teacher/avenging angel rolled into one. But she also notices that while the guys may get yelled at, they also get high fives. One new guy quickly becomes part of the sexual banter. It's bro culture in there, and she's clearly not a player.

Welcome to the world of women.

And that's exactly where our journey as men needs to start.

When I first started hearing stories like these years ago, my initial thought was to try to explain them away. I knew there was a lot of sexism out there, but I tended to think only of the most blatant cases. Once a woman friend told me about a male supervisor laying on the sexual innuendos like a bricklayer slaps down mortar. I was disgusted and started dishing out advice. It was well-meaning, but I didn't have a clue. I didn't have a clue why that man felt entitled to make those comments and I didn't have a clue why it would be hard for my friend, a smart and strong woman, to make him stop.

Luckily, around that time one woman gave me some really good advice. It's advice that goes to the heart of what men who are embracing gender equality must do. She said: "We appreciate that you're concerned about sexism. But if you really want to support us, if you really want to help bring about change, then you've got to start by listening harder to what we have to say."

"What if I disagree?" I asked.

"That's fine. You don't need to agree with everything I say, but you need to listen."

"Okay."

"One of the problems we're up against is that men have long monopolized the airwaves. Men have been the voices of authority in our places of worship. In higher education. In politics, the media, arts, and science. This doesn't make men bad," she said. "And sometimes those who've had their voices heard most have been totally caring and wonderful men. The problem is that monopoly. Having a monopoly on what is said and who has a voice of authority gives you power to be heard even more. And that power in turn gives you more authority. That power has given men more money and resources than women. That type of power is what a male-dominated society is all about."

Listening can prove tricky. At times it's hard not to feel under attack. Generalizations by some women don't help. *Men always do [such and such]*, or *Men are such [whatevers]*. We think, *No, I know a lot of men who don't always do that, perhaps never, and I know many men who don't fit that stereotype.*

It's easy to get your back up, but as men, we've got to remember we're hearing a distillation of anger, frustrations, concerns, sadness, and personal truths that has crystallized over a lifetime. Think about those vignettes at the beginning of the chapter. It's not like this happens once in a lifetime; this stuff is relentless. One of the things that surprised so many men when #MeToo exploded was the extent that violence—from almost mundane forms of sexual harassment at work to outright sexual and physical attacks at work, on the streets, and at home—was a recurring feature of so many women's lives. That's why men need to listen without instantly shooting back, "I'm not like that." If you're not like that, she doesn't need to be told. We need to wait our turn to speak, to ask more questions. We need to listen with respect and intention.

When we stick with listening, we start making discoveries. (Of course, when I say "discoveries," it's kind of like saying that Columbus discovered America. Sure he did, except for the millions of people who'd been living here for the previous ten or twenty thousand years.) What I really mean is that by listening to some of the 3.5 billion people on the planet who already know this stuff, we start looking at the world differently. We start discovering new things ourselves. We learn how to connect the experiences of women to our own experiences as a man.

For me, I discovered a world that had been hidden to me. I realized that when I listened to women speak, it was like reading the books that hadn't been written, hearing the political proclamations that hadn't been made, contemplating the sermons that hadn't been spoken, witnessing the scientific discoveries and inventions that either never happened or that had to wait to be announced until a man came along. These things hadn't happened, or hadn't happened nearly in proportion to the percentage of women on the planet, because of the barriers my half had put on women for the past eight or ten thousand years. Girls and women denied an education. Denied the vote. Denied a place of authority in our religions. Up against barriers in the workplace. They were expected to have sole responsibility for the never-ending tasks of housework and child rearing. Far too many were silenced by violence.

I heard much that, as a man, really pissed me off—at some of my brothers for suppressing women's voices and women's truths, and at myself for the ways I remained stuck in the rigid definitions of manhood and for behaving, at least at times, in thoughtless ways in relation to women I cared about.

Privilege and Other Revelations
from Listening

I remember one beautiful autumn day. I took a walk in the park. The sky was deep blue and the trees were orange, red, and yellow. For hours I walked, feeling good to be alive.

The next day I ran into my wise friend Varda Burstyn. I was still floating from my day in the park and I launched into my rhapsody: The trees! The sky! The fresh autumn air! All the while she just stared at me. Finally I said, "What?"

Varda said, "I too took a walk in a park yesterday. Here's what happened to me." And she proceeded to tell how a man started following her. He never came close, but as she turned down one wooded path and then another, he was never far behind. She headed to more open space. She saw two men sitting on a park bench having an animated conversation. As she drew near, they stopped talking. And, checking her out from head to toe, they stared as she walked past. Later, a couple of men whistled at her.

What for me had been a basic right—that is, to take a walk in the park—was for her an experience of harassment and intimidation.

So I did what any decent guy would do: I apologized. I said I was sorry she had to endure that. I apologized on behalf of all mankind.

But Varda said, "Why are you apologizing? Did you harass me? Did you harass someone in the park? Did you see harassment taking place and not do something?"

"No . . . but . . ."

"But nothing. I don't want you to feel guilty for something you didn't do. I want you to feel angry. Angry that a woman in your city doesn't have the same basic rights that you have."

I nodded.

"And I want you to know all this is about the privilege you enjoy as a man."

Privilege. Now there's a word.

Sure, I knew because I came from a middle-class family, because my parents had put me through university, I was privileged.

Having lived in North Carolina in the days of racial segregation, I knew I was privileged as a white person.

I knew that as a person now living in Canada I was privileged to enjoy a healthcare system, public safety, and a standard of living that people in much of the world could only dream about.

But she was talking about something else.

She was talking about layers of privilege that had been invisible to me.

And that's the thing about privilege. Some of the most profound forms of privilege that we men have traditionally enjoyed are invisible to us. Or, to paraphrase anti-racist educator Peggy McIntosh, privilege is an invisible knapsack full of bargaining chips that give you unearned credibility and keys that let you unlock doors that others have a harder time walking through.[2]

As a man, I don't have to think about going into a job interview and having someone wonder how soon I'm going to take a year off to look after my kids (even though, as we'll see in our chapter on fatherhood, that's exactly what more and more men are doing these days).

I don't have to fret that my ideas will be brushed off because I'm part of the supposedly irrational half of the species or because just maybe I'm having my period.

I won't have my boss assume I can't go on a work trip because I'd have to be away from my family, or go to a job site because it might be too dangerous, or sit down in a negotiation because the people on the other side are from a country where women aren't taken seriously.

And I won't ever have to worry that some well-funded, well-organized groups will make sure that politicians pass laws that force me to carry a child in my own body when I don't wish to do so, or tell me I can't access contraception to prevent myself from becoming pregnant.

Privilege isn't only about what you have and what you get to enjoy. It's about not having to think about those things. It's about not even knowing you have those things.

This understanding of privilege opens the door to much more. We begin to understand both the subtle and blatant ways that privilege gets conferred because of our sex, sexual orientation, gender orientation, the color of our skin, our religion, economic class, physical abilities, age, or what country we were born in. We come to realize that our experiences are shaped by moments pinging away at us from birth. This happens so much that feminist thinkers no longer simply talk about women's and men's experiences, but of how many forms of hierarchy, privilege, and unequal power intersect in our own lives. You might have privilege as a man, but you don't because you're African American. You have it because you're straight, but you don't because you're Muslim in Trump's America. This isn't to come up with some bizarre rankings of who has it worse—say, how does a middle-class, bisexual woman in Tokyo stack up against a formerly middle-class straight man from Syria who is living in a refugee camp in Jordan? But rather it's to appreciate the complexity of our experiences and relationships and to develop better approaches for bringing about change.

And so, listening to the voices of women has a way of exploding complacency. The point of listening is to allow men to understand and experience some of the anger that women (or certain groups of men) feel. It's a way to understand the direction that our workplaces, our families, our countries need to go in order to create a world that is safer, more just, and more prosperous. It's a way of helping release pent-up brilliance, pent-up ideas, pent-up leadership, pent-up strength. It's a way of improving our relationships.

The World through the Eyes of Women

If men were to view the world from a woman's perspective, here's some of what we would see: The persistent income gap between women and men. The clustering of women into certain (lower-paid) occupations. The barriers to advancement women still face in the corporate world. The double dose of discrimination experienced by women of color and women of ethnic and religious minorities. The piddling representation of women in elected office and the judiciary. The sexual, physical, and emotional violence a large number of women experience. The chasm between the amount of time women spend on housework and childcare compared to men on average, even in many families where both have full-time jobs outside the home. The lack of family-friendly work policies, quality childcare, and parental leave, the absence of which still disproportionately zaps women. The higher rates of poverty women experience. Second-class citizenship within many religions. Men who continue to enforce control over women's bodies by using their political and religious clout to restrict access to birth control and abortion. Mile-high barriers that still exist in much of the world to girls' education.

And that's only the short version of a very long list. As painful as it is to hear about, we men need to hear it. So we can influence our friends, our coworkers, our teammates, and our sons. So we can challenge the claims of those men (and women) who still oppose women's rights or who think that we've now entered a postfeminist utopia. So we can rethink how we raise boys to be men. So we can honestly examine our own biases, attitudes, and behaviors that might be part of the problem, but also so we can strengthen our gender-equitable attitudes and behaviors. So we can take action in our own lives.

We men need to be able to recognize the toll of discrimination, biases, violence, and out-and-out oppression that women face. We need to have as clear an idea as possible what all these things look like and how they affect so many spheres of women's lives and, by extension, our lives.

Women should be able to count on us to be informed, fearless, and tireless advocates of equality and justice when we're in a meeting at work, when we're in our homes, our classrooms and places of worship, and polling booths. We've got to know this stuff if we are going to be at their side as leaders of change.

But we also need to know one additional thing, and this is a piece of remarkable news for men. It may sound strange, but it turns out that men pay a terrible price for the very ways we define manhood and construct men's lives within societies where we have more power. We need to uncover this paradox at the heart of our lives, because in it lies some of the deepest reasons why men can fully stand beside women as partners for change.

It turns out that the gender equality revolution will mean that our lives as men will be changed for the better too.

3

MEN'S LIVES IN A MALE-DOMINATED WORLD

The most wonderful moment of my life was when my child was born.

It was at that moment, just seconds after the birth, that the nurse spoke. Until that moment, she talked in her normal voice, but then her voice dropped an octave and she said, "It's a boy. What a strong little fellow."

I was shocked.

Not because it was a boy. I kind of figured there was a fifty-fifty chance of that. I was shocked by how she said it, her voice far lower than his would be for another thirteen years.

I knew that if it had been a girl, the nurse's voice would have ascended to squeaky heights and she would have said something like, "What a sweet little thing."

It was true, he was a strong little fellow, but as far as I was concerned, he was also the sweetest thing that had ever squirmed its way onto the planet. Yet here he was, just seconds old, and he was being fitted for a football jersey. It was like the word *man* was being stamped on his delicately wrinkled forehead.

And that's what happens to us all, females and males. That very same story is happening in delivery rooms across the country and around the world. From an early age we are held differently, talked to differently, dressed in different clothes, and given different toys. Children are bombarded by our society's definitions of what it means to be a boy or a girl.

Traditionally, at least, boys and girls carried ready-made baggage. It wasn't so long ago that girls were expected to be gentle, delicate, compliant, emotional—little princesses. I was going to say that so much has changed, and in a way it has. Particularly since the late 1960s, as women have challenged limiting ideals of femininity and women's second-class status, the repertoire and aspirations of girls has greatly expanded. Yet a steady pink diet remains a grinding reality in the lives of girls. Indeed, as women leaders in the workplace or politics often discover, they're damned if they stick to the old stereotypes and damned if they break from them and assert their power as women.

Although the emotional space for men has enlarged a bit in recent years—I mean, I'm glad that men can finally hug, even if we have to pound the crap out of each other's backs as we do so—boys are still expected to be robust, tough, strong, risk takers and, perhaps most of all, creatures who don't succumb to any feelings that are deemed a sign of weakness.[1]

Children pick up on these messages remarkably early. Partly it's because from infancy on we're amazing mimics. In fact, we even have a type of nerve cell called mirror neurons that reward us for echoing the emotions of those around us.

I often hear parents say, "Wait a minute, I've had a boy and I've had a girl and I know there is a difference in their behavior."

There was an experiment that tested this. Observers were each given a baby to play with. Half were boys, half were girls. The observers made notes about the infants' behaviors. Then the babies were taken away; new babies were brought in. This was repeated with new groups of observers and new babies. Finally, researchers fed the observations into the computer and, lo and behold, the boys indeed were louder, more aggressive, and used more large muscle movement. The girls were more delicate, quieter, and better behaved. It seemed to confirm all our assumptions.

The only problem was that the observers were being fooled. Indeed, half the babies were boys and half girls, but each time the babies were taken away, they were randomly dressed in boys' or girls' clothing and then the same babies were brought back out. In other words, if you were an observer, you didn't know if that cute thing in the pink dress or the rugged dungarees was a girl or a boy. But most important, you didn't know you didn't know.

The researchers kept track, and when they compared the

observations to the actual biological sex of the babies, they found there was no correlation with the observed behavior.

So why did the observers think they saw a clear male-female difference? One reason is that we see what we expect to see. That's how all stereotyping works. A person might do ten different things as we watch them, but we tend to notice and remember the things that conform to our assumptions about that group. So a pink dress supposedly meant it was a girl and this in turn meant certain behaviors were noticed, and vice versa for boys.[2]

But it gets more complicated. The other reason they saw differences was that we interact with girls and boys differently. One day a friend was standing at a bus stop with her baby. The baby was dressed in a lumberjack outfit, you know, one of those red-and-black check shirts that lumberjacks copied from hipsters. A casual friend came up. This was his first news about the baby and he enthusiastically took the baby, started tossing it into the air, and then enthusiastically proclaimed, "What a bruiser. What's his name?"

My friend said, "*Her* name is Sarah."

And without missing a beat, he cuddled her and gently stroked her head.

These are learning experiences for the baby. That "boy" is learning to be a risk taker and take pleasure at physical thrills. The "girl," in spite of the changes in our era, is still getting taught that she is delicate and needs to be looked after.

The truth is that children need both these things, boisterous play and gentle cuddling. But we still dish it out unevenly. And so we learn different things.

Celery and Brain Development

This learning is not intellectual. It's not as if the baby is thinking, *I must conform to gender stereotypes*. Rather it is part of the rapid development of our brains. Every single day, an infant is creating millions of new neural connections. At birth, our brains are only 10 percent developed. I don't mean 10 percent of their adult size. I mean they lack the complex entanglement of neurons and synapses; whole regions that constitute our adult brains are barely there.

It reminds me of the experiment we did in elementary school. We put a stick of celery in colored water and a day or two later the celery had sucked up the color. Admittedly, it's a very simplistic comparison, but our rapidly developing brains react to, absorb, and become structured through the relationship with the surrounding social and natural environments. This is truer for humans than other animals in part because we are totally dependent on parents for a substantially longer period. We soak up the colored water for a very long time.

All those moments of play, being talked to differently, and carefully observing the world become the nurturing environment within which we build our brains. And since this is happening in a male-dominated society where gender really matters, this is a process where we internalize gender expectations, ideals, relations—gender power—right into our brains. We don't simply learn to fit a stereotype; our brains become *gendered*.

By *gender* I'm not referring to whether we are male or female. Our sex is a biological reality that describes our place in the process of reproduction and physically locates most, although not all, humans. (And scientists, in part recognizing a range of genetic variations but also challenged by the coming out of many trans people, are acknowledging that we're not as clearly split into two sexes as once thought.) Gender, on the other hand, has to do with our ideas and ideals of manhood and womanhood, masculinity and femininity. Gender is about the relations of power between the sexes.

In other words, it's not correct to talk about "the male brain" or "the female brain." Just as our chromosomes are 98.6 percent identical between a male and a female, we are not born with marked brain differences.[3] Rather, nature and nurture collide and coincide: Our nature is that our brains are plastic, malleable; our nature is also that we humans are wholly dependent on adults for many years. During that time, we form deep and powerful emotional attachments to those adults while our brains develop during a painstakingly long and slow process. This process of development is happening within a social setting, one that, at least for now, is still divided and defined by gender. Nature is what allows our brains to become gendered; society is what contributes the gendered template that shapes our identities, our sense of self, and more.

It's not nature versus nurture—that's an outmoded debate. Rather, it's nature and nurture collaborating to create men and women, the masculine and feminine, you and me.

Although I say "masculine and feminine," there are more than two genders. In fact, gender ideals and definitions vary from era to era and culture to culture. Individuals integrate, react to, reject, and modify these gender definitions in their own ways.[4] My self-definition of manhood, my sense of self, the ways I integrate men's power into that self, and the forms of privilege I enjoy as a white, urban, middle-class, educated, Jewish, straight, North American man born in the 1950s is different from a young, black, gay, working-class man who lives up the street or a poor, rural, white, male farmer who lives only an hour away. And, increasingly, more individuals are coming forward and saying the confines of our traditional assumptions of who should be defined as male or female simply don't fit them at all.

Where Do These Ideas of Manhood Come From?

The immediate answer is that we're born into a hailstorm of images, messages, and more. Some are blatant: walk into a large toy store and there's a Berlin Wall dividing the girls' and boys' toys. Some messages are subtle but have an impact: watch cars driving by, and if there is a man and woman in the front seat, chances are it's the man driving. This sends a message to the impressionable little minds in the back seat that it takes a man to wield this huge piece of machinery, and if a man and woman are together, the man should be in charge—all this in spite of the fact that, statistically, women are better drivers. Start looking at the world through gendered lenses—note the images in the media, watch who takes up more public space, who speaks with voices of authority, who does what jobs—and your view of the world will never be the same.

But this begs a question. Ultimately, where do our gender ideas and, more specifically, our ideas about manhood come from? It's not like there was a board of directors of men who decided the rules of manliness and femininity. Oh wait, there was—from groups of religious authorities, to traditionally all-male government bodies, to the clubs of men who invented modern sports culture around the beginning of the twentieth century. These groups of men created, codified, and justified the rules governing manhood and womanhood (and made sure that those who broke them were penalized).[5]

Simply put, our ideals about manhood emerge from and reinforce the realities of patriarchy, a male-dominated society.

Get off the plane in Lisbon, Portugal. Rent a car. Drive southeast for a couple of hours, and you'll reach the walled town of Évora. But it's the surrounding countryside that really brought me there, for it is a site of extensive human settlements and monuments built from 5000 to 3000 BCE.

The earlier monuments are reminiscent of Stonehenge, the circles in the Orkney Islands, and the standing stones of Brittany, except that here they aren't as towering as some of those. They line up to mark the summer solstice and the spring and fall equinoxes. The monuments are early Neolithic, built when humans first domesticated crops and animals. Our ancestors must have created these monuments to follow the seasons that were now so important to their survival. The magnitude of the monuments—the carvings into the rock, their careful placement in sockets chipped deep into the bedrock—suggests a profound worship of the cosmos and the mysteries of nature. But there is also a sense of humans now mastering nature; these stones appear to be a monument to this mastery. Carved into some of the stones is the image of a shepherd's crook—a symbol of control over nature, a symbol wielded by pharaohs and one that still carries religious meaning, for it is the staff the pope carries. Shepherds indeed care for their flock, but there is no question who is ultimately in control.

These early Neolithic years were a time of social transition. Humans in these parts were starting to dominate nature but likely living in fairly equitable societies. Only a few kilometers away, but hundreds of years later, we see the signs of change. Likely dating back to about 4000 to 3000 BCE, there are burial monuments constructed with gigantic stone slabs twenty-six feet tall, laboriously shaped and carried here and erected into circular rooms over the course of dozens of years. And who was buried inside? They had three characteristics. Only a few were entombed, showing that humans had developed a society where a few had power over the many and those few appropriated far more of what the society produced, as witnessed by the tremendous time and energy that went into producing their tombs. Second, the bodies were all men. And the third? They had weapons—these were societies where men had learned to use violence not merely to hunt but to fight.

Many anthropologists figure that for most of the two hundred thousand years humans like us have been around, we tended to live in small, equitable groups of people who foraged to survive. Sure, there were different tasks that males and females did, occasioned by the fact that a female spent a significant part of her short adult life pregnant or breastfeeding, which kept her more bound to their settlements. (This also meant that females likely played a disproportionate role in the greatest technological revolution in human history, the Neolithic revolution when humans domesticated animals and cultivated plants.) But a division of labor didn't confer hierarchy. As a generalized rule, likely starting about eight or ten thousand years ago (although unevenly in different parts of the world) hierarchal, male-dominated societies emerged.

Philosopher Mary O'Brien speculated in her imaginative book *The Politics of Reproduction*[6] that patriarchy emerged, at least in part, as a way for men to control women's fertility and the process of reproduction, in the same way that humans were learning to control nature. Or at least we can say that fundamental to men's control and inheritance of land and animals in their own clan or tribe was their control over women's lives. The extent to which we still assume that men are the rational half of humanity and females the ones linked to irrational surges of nature seems to attest to this. And the extent to which certain groups of men still seem hell-bent on controlling women's reproduction—think of the injunction against birth control and abortion among religious fundamentalists of all stripes—means that the imperative of controlling women's bodies has lasted to this day.

So when we define masculinity as about having power *over* women, *over* nature, *over* other men, and *over* one's own unruly emotions, it is a definition of manhood that reflects a social reality. Once it emerges, it feels totally natural. We assume it's just the way men are.

Scientists have a growing understanding of how social experiences and realties actually shape our nature. The plasticity of our brains allows them to change and develop based on our experiences.[7] And this is also the field of epigenetics. It seems that things that happen to us can actually change our nature. Or, to put it differently, our nature isn't as fixed as scientists once thought. Your DNA code is fixed, but stress and diet and how we live can shape which genes get down to work and which ones are there only as a potential. Our environment and what we're doing day-to-day can turn genes off and on. (Later we'll see how this affects men if they become fathers.) The lives we live as men, along with the pressures and stress we experience to "be a man," cause changes in a complex cascade of hormones. Our nature as humans is that our nature is mutable. One way it mutates is that gendered expectations and relationships get locked right into our brains.

Beyond Bad Habits

I have a habit that drives my wife, Betty, crazy. I talk to strangers. Standing in line at supermarket checkouts, on elevators, and walking down the street. I sometimes find out interesting things and, best of all, it helps me feel connected with the world.

One day I am waiting to do a keynote at a conference. I've wandered into the hallway and am about to return to the conference room when I notice a janitor staring through a window on the door that looks into the room.

I say hello.

He asks what the conference is about.

I say it's about women's empowerment, promoting gender equality, and challenging men's power.

He snorts. Not nastily, but enough to let me know he doesn't buy it.

"It's a good thing," I protest. "Equality."

"You didn't hear me say it wasn't."

I wait.

"But power?" he says. "Are you kidding me? I don't have power. I don't make enough money. My boss treats me like dirt. I'm driving a car held together by duct tape. The government tells me what to do. My minister tells me what to do. My wife tells me what to do. My kids tell me what to do. My damn dog tells me what to do."

How do we square these comments with the assertion that we live in a society where men have more power than women?

Understanding the Janitor

There are several possible explanations for the reactions of the janitor.

Explanation One: He's pissed off at women and feminism. However, I don't get that impression. He says he isn't

grumbling against equality. In fact, as we talk more, he tells me about his two daughters and how he wants the best for them.

Explanation Two: Real progress has taken place in terms of women's rights and gender equality. And so he doesn't buy the argument that women still face discrimination. Think about it. In the days of your mother or grandmother, there were enormous barriers to women's education in most of the world. (Sadly, this is still the case in parts of Africa and Asia.) Now, in North America, Europe, and parts of Latin America and Asia, women are the majority of undergraduate students; women were the majority at the medical school my daughter-in-law attended. In the days of your mother or grandmother, women in the United States couldn't open their own bank account without their husband's signature. Violence against women was barely ever mentioned. There has been progress—and all of it a testament to the fortitude of women pushing for change. But this is only part of the explanation for the janitor's words.

Explanation Three: The janitor, dazzled by this progress, hasn't noticed the many ways that women remain second-class citizens in much of the world. Or how, even in countries like our own, women still lag behind. And he might not have noticed that bald-faced biases still exist.

Explanation Four: Forms of power and privilege the janitor does enjoy are largely invisible to him. (The privilege we discussed in the previous chapter.)

Explanation Five: Male-dominated societies are not only ones where men as a group have power over women. Some

men also have power over other men; some groups of men are more highly valued. This janitor is a low-paid working-class man doing a low-prestige job. He experiences powerlessness himself. As a man at the bottom of the economic ladder, he isn't exactly cashing out on the benefits of being a man. As such, the janitor's words reflect a certain reality: he actually doesn't have much power. So one reason why many men feel they don't have power is that, in relation to at least some or even many other men and some women, they actually don't have much social or economic power. Some men, because of the color of their skin or the country where they were born or their religion or sexual orientation or physical differences or economic class, face enormous discrimination and oppression. There definitely are a few men who have far more social, political, and economic power than others. And, increasingly, there are some women who have more social, political, and economic power than many men, although those women still, in many ways, experience oppression.

All these are pretty good explanations for the janitor's reaction. But there's another reason. Deeper and more hidden. A thing that takes us right to the heart of men's lives.

The Paradox of Men's Power

Gender is a social construction formed by taking the full range of human possibilities and splitting them right down the middle. This division defines a list as diverse as clothes preferences to hairstyles to the ability to operate certain machines or do certain jobs to the ability to lead others in pol-

itics or religious observance to whether one is supposed to be nurturing to . . . well, the list is pretty much endless. Not only have we traditionally assigned one-half of human attributes and abilities to each sex, but we also say that the other half is off limits to the other sex. Thus from birth on, our society limits the individuality of each and every one of us.

And woe be it to him or her who steps across the divide and reclaims attributes or interests they're not supposed to have.

Among the many great gains by women in recent years is the insistence that they shouldn't be trapped within one side of this great divide.

And, of course, one of the tired and stupid old stereotypes about gay men is that they are supposed to be effeminate; that is, they have crossed the line. Not only is this untrue—in the sense that gay men show pretty much the same range in personalities as straight men—but the notion has an even deeper problem. It suggests that some of the attributes traditionally associated with women (such as being able to express emotions or care about one's health and appearance) would be degrading if men were to exhibit them, when, in fact, the opposite is true.

Thus, for all men, manhood gets defined not only by what a man is supposed to be, but even more so by what he's *not* supposed to be. For example, it's not only that a man is supposed to always be strong and courageous; he's supposed to have no weakness or fear. Not only is he supposed to be rugged and hardy, he's supposed to be reckless about his health, safety, and well-being. All the while, he's supposed to stand alone, to take stoically what life throws at him without complaint.

No man can live up to this. You can't always be strong and fearless, have all the answers, be the economic provider, be ready and able to fight, be good with tools, good at sports, talking, and drinking, and fit seamlessly into the tight suit of manhood. Oh yeah, and we're not supposed to show too many emotions; hell, in many cultures, we're not even supposed to have emotions except perhaps for anger. Not just a suit. A suit of armor. No man can pull it off.

Perhaps you'd think we'd be able to live up to most of this. For one thing, there is a system of rewards and punishments ready to encourage us. The boy or young man who seems to live up to such things is greatly rewarded: he is the captain of the football team, he is popular, and he "gets" the beautiful girl. Meanwhile, the boy who doesn't fit in suffers: he isn't popular, he is bullied and teased, and he is beat up. This is virtually all the growing boy sees around him; it is what he is exposed to, it is the heroic and strong image of the athletes he watches on TV, it is the coolness of the rock star, it is the swagger and apparent confidence of the older boys, it is the authority of his father and other grown men. He has many models to emulate. More than that, because these ideals surround him, they feel natural, not simply the alpha versions of manhood, but the illusion that every man he sees seems to fit into these images. Ideals that embody the power that children of course do not have. It is seductive beyond belief.

What's more, we don't just learn to act a certain way, in

the sense of consciously learning a thing and parking that thing as a guidepost in our brains. Rather, as we saw earlier, we internalize those external social realities right into our developing brains. So, again, you'd think we'd have it all locked in tight.

But the truth remains: we cannot live up to all those expectations.

Male-dominated societies have created expectations and ideals for men that set boys and men up for failure.

Male-dominated societies have determined that men should not be emotionally aware or expressive—or at least, not *too* expressive—and, as a result, have made us and those around us completely vulnerable to deeply rooted and, often, deeply hidden emotions.

Male-dominated societies have indeed brought huge rewards for half of humanity, but the very ways we have defined that world of men's power is a death trap for men ourselves.

Male-dominated societies have divvied up those rewards very unequally among men.

Men have a big stake in bringing that world of gender inequality to an end.[8]

Resistance and Changing Ideals of Manhood

A woman in Ohio told me a story. Her about-to-be-five-year-old wanted pink pajamas for Christmas. You see, pink was his favorite color. She'd already mentioned this to her husband, who wasn't happy about it. She didn't think it was a big deal that her boy liked pink, although she was worried he might get teased at kindergarten the following year. But she went ahead and bought him pink pajamas, which he opened with total delight. The boy's grandmother was visiting and expressed horror. "Those are girl's pajamas," she told him. "You don't want those." The little boy looked crestfallen but didn't say a word. That is, until the grandmother was leaving. She was at the front door tucked into her winter coat when the little boy marched up to her and said, "Pink is still my favorite color."

So, back to the stick of celery soaking up the colored water. We can see why it's an inadequate description of how our brains become gendered. Even as children, we're not passive recipients of the messages of society. True, those have an impact. But so does our temperament and personality. So does loving support that sends us a different message.

And so does resistance to the narrow demands placed on us from birth. It's not just that we can't live up to all the expectations placed on us. These days, an increasing number of boys and men don't want to live up to those limiting, self-defeating expectations. Nor do we want to define ourselves in opposition to the skills and qualities that women have nurtured over the eons. As one young man told me, "I felt ripped off, I mean really ripped off, when I realized the job that had been done on me."

Despite all the constant and pulverizing messages that boys and men receive about manhood, despite the rewards we get for being "real men," despite teasing and bullying, boys and men have often found ways to resist the demands a male-dominated society imposes on us and men impose on ourselves. I've often figured that's why many men are much better as grandfathers than they were as fathers. It's not simply they have more time; it's that their priorities have shifted. It's because many men, by the time they've reached their fifties and sixties, have abandoned the ruthless pursuit of a certain brand of manhood.

I've heard older men say with enormous regret, "I worked my whole life for my career and I said it was for my family. Now I'm retired, so I don't have the rewards that go with my job, but now my kids are grown up and I don't even know them." There's enormous tragedy in that—but *that* was because of the privilege we gave him as a man. Back in his day, he probably didn't equally share the hard-slogging, day-in, day-out work of changing diapers, making lunches, and looking after the house and the immediate needs of those within it. He was able to pursue his career, hobbies, or education; he was able to relax in front of the TV or go out with friends at night. But, paradoxically, the very thing that gave him rewards is the source of his pain. And often those very men are the ones who embrace grandfatherhood or community volunteer work with a passion. They now realize that the real values of human life are not the car or the title but our relationships with those we love.

Across the country and around the world, we are now seeing a rapidly growing number of men who reject the narrow demands of manhood and who reject the notion of male superiority to women. We see more men who are willing to be affectionate with their male friends. We see more men with close friendships with women and who show immense respect for female coworkers and colleagues. We see many men who are embracing a dramatic transformation in their role as fathers.

We see more men able to acknowledge their vulnerabilities and think about their health. I asked an offensive tackle from the NFL about concussions and whether he still followed the old code of playing through pain no matter what the consequences. "No way," he said. "Playing football pays good, but in the years ahead, I want to be able to play with my daughter."

We are also seeing more men who can openly and proudly declare their love and desire for other men, and in many parts of the world, we're seeing much greater acceptance about the diversity and flux of human desire. The forward movement in the past few years of LGBTQ rights, in celebration of diverse relationships, in winning same-sex marriage rights in more and more countries, and in a growing acceptance and welcome of trans individuals (although much remains to be done) are all, in part, about the rejection of the narrow straitjacket imposed by traditional gender norms that split human experience into an either/or equation and dictate that humans are supposedly on one side of the line or the other. Like the binary language of a computer, we're supposed to be either 0 or 1. But now, like the experimental quantum computers, you can be 0, 1, or both simultaneously. Or none of the above. None of us need be confined, limited, molded, manhandled, suppressed, or repressed by a binary gender definition and by binary power relationships.

Who can men thank for these many different changes in our lives?

In many cases, it is the inspiration and the challenge of feminist movements; it's the invitation by strong women in our own lives to join them in embracing a world of new possibilities. Men in the millions aren't spontaneously discovering they're great as caregivers and can find satisfaction doing the tough, day-in, day-out work of parenting. It's because we were pushed and challenged by women to do our share of the work.

All men are indebted to other movements of human liberation. Anti-racism struggles, such as the civil rights movement and the anti-apartheid fight in South Africa, showed all men and women that we have a collective capacity to change social values and institutions (as well as making us painfully aware of the ongoing barriers to change). These social movements celebrated values of equality. But they also showed that change isn't just handed to anyone. Societies have a sad way of perpetuating themselves; old attitudes and old ways have a tenacious hold, and those who benefit from the status quo have a great desire to keep things just as they are.

And *all* men owe a debt of gratitude to the gay liberation movements of the 1970s and '80s and the LGBTQ movements of today. These movements do more than celebrate the possibility for people to define who they desire and love. They also say that all of us can escape the limitations of our dominant and limiting ideas of gender and discover who we really are. In fact, if we were to pinpoint one group of men who, more than any other, opened the door for all men to look after themselves, think about their bodies in more positive ways, and allow for more genuinely close friendships with other men, it's gay men.

The past few decades have seen the start of an extraordinary and powerful shift. I don't claim that most men would self-identify as feminists, although an increasing number do. But if you go through many of the goals of feminism—equal right to an education, equal pay, equal access to jobs at all levels, ending sexual harassment at work and violence against women in the home—it's pretty clear that a solid majority of men are on our side. We can put numbers on these changes. In 1977, for example, 74 percent of US men thought that it's better for everyone if men earn the money while women take care of home and children. By 2008, just thirty years later, this had dropped to 40 percent. The latter percentage was almost identical to women's views—which shows not only that we still have a ways to go for everyone to embrace gender-equitable ideas, but also that there is a growing convergence between men's and women's views on issues that were once seen as "only" women's issues.[9]

In a similar vein, I don't need to argue that feminism *will be* good for boys and men. The dividends are already being racked up. Particularly among younger men, we're seeing an escape from some of the treacherous, self-harming, and homophobic ideals of manhood. Colleagues at my Washington, D.C., and Rio de Janeiro–based institute, Promundo (where I am a senior fellow) did a study of a representative sample of men aged eighteen to thirty in the United States, United

Kingdom, and Mexico. They showed a remarkable defiance of ideals of manhood that were the norm only a generation or two ago (and they belie the machismo stereotype about Mexican men).[10]

I agree that . . .	US	UK	Mexico
. . . it's not good for a boy to be taught to cook, sew, clean house, or take care of younger children.	28%	31%	17%
. . . a gay guy is not a "real man."	29%	30%	23%
. . . a "real man" would never say no to sex.	28%	31%	26%
. . . men should use violence to get respect, if necessary.	23%	25%	10%
. . . a man should always have the final say in decisions in his relationship or marriage.	34%	33%	21%

Nonetheless, it would be delusional to overstate men's support for gender equality, for there remains a significant backlash against feminism. There are so-called men's rights activists who claim the pendulum has shifted, who think it's now men like them who are the real victims, and who troll women who speak out for women's rights. There are religious fundamentalists—Christian, Jewish, Muslim, and Hindu—

who are hell-bent on reversing women's gains and reasserting men's power over women's bodies, women's behavior, and women's comings and goings. There are legislators and well-funded lobbyists who are working hard to enact legislation that will lead to women's deaths from needing to attain back-alley abortions, to more unwanted pregnancies (by restricting young people's access to birth control and comprehensive sex education), or to the victimization of LGBTQ people because of whom they love. And there are many other men who have been fed confusing or deceitful information about the goals of feminism, or who simply haven't had access to sound arguments in favor of gender equality. Indeed we do have a ways to go.

It would also be disingenuous to claim that feminism represents a simple, positive direction for men. If so, the walls of patriarchy would have tumbled a long time ago. As a group, boys and men still receive many tangible benefits from a fifty-fifty roll of the dice at conception. We don't call it privilege for nothing. And it's not simply about privilege; it's about the sheer emotional difficulty of change. It might be positive to ditch the armor of manhood, but without it you can be left feeling pretty vulnerable. What's more, it means holding yourself to account for your own past actions.

And yet, a rapidly increasing number of men are embracing gender equality. Men are starting to challenge each other and challenge themselves. Men are speaking out in support of women's rights and marching in the streets. And men are embracing changes in what it means to be a man not only because it's good for the women they care about, but also because it's good for themselves.

Change has happened, yes. But big challenges remain. Some of the biggest are in our workplaces.

4

THE NEW 9 TO 5

Pushing Hard for a Gender-Equal Economy

The goal of gender equality and the critical task of men counting ourselves in is nowhere more clearly seen than in the workplace. All these problems start with a gender-inequitable economy: Unequal pay. Job ghettoes. Lack of work-life balance. Missing or inadequate parental leave. Barriers to promotion and advancement. Sexual harassment. And workplace culture that holds women back, slices into productivity, and has negative consequences for men as well.

Imagine a worldwide economy. It's a combination of all the factories and stores, the offices, farms, and mines, the transportation networks and financial institutions. It's the hospitals and schools, the day care centers and nursing homes. It's the government departments and the state structures that provide the framework for business and commerce to function. It's the rules and regulations that keep the whole thing ticking and, at times, the police and judges who make sure rules are followed.

And there are whole parts of the economy that we don't measure, such as the work of looking after our homes and raising our children. How we arrange such matters is part of the overall economic structure of a society. This is the place where we raise the next generation of workers and where, day in and day out, we recharge and re-create—hence the word *recreation*—our capacity to work.

Even sticking to paid employment for the moment, imagine all the people, billions of us, in all these places of work.

And now imagine the impact if a whole swath of people have a hundred roadblocks keeping them from full participation in this economy. Think of not only how they must feel or the impact on their individual lives and families, but also the costs to the economy as a whole.

Our economies include barriers that have greatly reduced women's participation, especially in full-time work. Show me a part-time worker, and most likely it's a woman. In the United States, for example, 64 percent of part-time workers are women, while 43 percent of full-time workers are women. Only among African Americans do we see a different pattern, where women represent 51 percent of black full-time workers (although women still comprise 63 percent of black part-time workers)[1]—this is partly about racist barriers to employment among African American men, including the staggering rate at which black men get locked into prison.

In Europe, on average, 56 percent of men have full-time employment compared to only 39 percent of women.[2]

Part-time work usually means jobs with lower hourly pay, fewer benefits, and less job security. Part-time work results in lower family income and less financial independence for women. Lower income results in a disproportionate number of women living in poverty. US Census Bureau statistics show that working-age women are 38 percent more likely to live in poverty than men.[3] Lower financial independence means many things, including a reduced ability to get out of bad or abusive relationships.

What has created this situation, both the unequal pay and the greater chance that a woman is working part-time? What are the barriers, subtle and blatant, institutional and attitudinal? First and foremost are the disproportionate demands on women to do domestic labor and childcare. You choose to do this work or do it by default, and you might not be able to take on a full-time paid job or go for that promotion or do overtime or get that extra training or education even if you wanted to.

Add to this the biases about who is suitable for certain jobs and which jobs are most valuable. There are lingering assumptions that men should be in the priority line when it comes to full-time work—and although this assumption has diminished in countries such as ours, it's still very much part of the international landscape. The barriers can come from laws and government policies, even including things as seemingly innocuous as tax laws in countries where a "second" income (understood as a woman's income) is taxed at a much higher rate than the primary income, thus being a disincentive to women getting paid work.

If we removed the barriers to women, if we had a society where women and men equally did full-time and part-time work and participated equally in the labor force, the economic gains would be staggering. The number crunchers at the McKinsey Global Institute estimate this would lead to a whopping $28 trillion gain to the international GDP by 2025. That's equal to the combined size of the current US and Chinese economies. It's a 26 percent increase in world GDP.[4] Although the gains would be highest where women's participation in full-time paid labor is lowest (such as in India, or Saudi Arabia, which makes India look like a feminist paradise), every country would be positively affected.

Women's equality in paid work isn't exactly chump change. The single biggest shot in the arm we can give to the world's economies is gender equality.

Getting the Measure on Gender Inequality at Work

Gender inequality is surprisingly easy to quantify, especially in a highly measured place like the economy.

Take how much people get paid.

Right now, half a century after the birth of the modern feminist movement, women working full-time in the United States are earning, on average, 82 cents for every buck that men make. In Canada, women on hourly wages working full-time earn 88 percent of what men make. In Europe, it is 84 percent. And in Japan, women earn 73 percent of what men make.[5]

Although in some cases unequal pay results literally from women getting paid less for doing exactly the same work, it's also because of job ghettoes—jobs and professions where we see disproportionate numbers of women or other groups with less social and economic power—and the way we've defined the value of work traditionally done by the latter. Think of the world of education. The highest-paid and most respected teachers are university professors, a profession traditionally dominated by men. A big notch down in pay and prestige are high school teachers, where the numbers are more closely balanced, although there are more women than men. Elementary school teachers are disproportionately women and traditionally paid less than high school teachers, although in some areas, unions have fought for and won equal pay with other teachers. Finally are day care "workers," who are often not even designated as teachers and are by far the lowest paid. They are overwhelmingly women. This discrepancy reflects what we value (work by men) and the things we devalue (matters we associate with women's caregiving role). This certainly is not about who contributes most to learning. In fact, it's absolutely reversed. Most of what we learn in our whole lives happens at a very young age, when most brain development occurs. And yet those who nurture and teach the young are the lowest paid. I greatly value the work of professors (and used to be one myself), but you could argue that the most important educators are the lowest paid and least respected because they do a job associated with and mainly done by women.

One interesting thing is that while women are increasingly cracking into some professions previously monopolized by men (medical doctors being one of the most dramatic examples), the reverse hasn't occurred (nurses are still predominantly women).

When you think about the causes of the pay gap—a history of sexist hiring practices, women historically having less higher education, women on average doing much more of the childcare and housework and being less able or interested in moving up the ladder, women being pressed into lower-paying job ghettoes, and women getting paid less for the same or comparable work—you'd hope that since we're making progress on at least some of those fronts, the pay gap would be shrinking. The good news is that this is true, and that's because women have been fighting for it. In the United States, back in 1979, women earned 62 percent of what men did, so 82 percent today shows a remarkable improvement and the impact of feminism.

But let me add the bad news: the rate of progress slowed down to a trickle in most countries more than a decade ago. At the current rate, pay received by women and men will become equal in England, for example, in 2069 according to the consulting firm Deloitte[6]—just in time for the children of my grandchildren to say "yippy!"

You'd hope the acceleration of women in higher education would do the trick. After all, in countries from the United States to Iran, more women are graduating from university then men. However, US women with a bachelor's degree receive only 77 percent of what their male counterparts make; with an advanced degree, it's even worse: 73 percent.[7] Young men popping out of college in this era of supposed equality are averaging $20.87 per hour for full-time work while their female counterparts are pulling in $17.88.[8]

What unequal pay means is that women in the United States and Australia, for example, need an additional forty-seven workdays a year to earn what men make. The result is that a male-female or female-female couple is going to have to work a lot longer to save for that new car or vacation. (This is the economic advantage a male-male couple enjoys: their average household income tends to be higher for the simple reason two men are bringing home the bacon.)

The Incredible Shrinking Woman

Even faced with these facts, some men will object. *I'll give it to you that things used to be really unequal,* they will say, *but now the tables have turned. Women now have all the advantages, and men are the ones constantly losing out.* Here's what I'd say to them:

First of all, in a gender-equal world a man will indeed lose out in employment or advancement or elections to a woman 50 percent of the time. But right now, at a time of change, because too many men feel entitled to be the Chosen Ones, having to suddenly share resources with women or compete with women feels like an unequivocal loss. After all, patriarchy has been an eight-thousand-year-long affirmative action program for men. Feminism proposes to cancel that program.

It's actually true that men are increasingly losing out in good employment. But it's not because of women. It's because we're undergoing a rapid shift in who benefits within our economy. We're seeing a concentration of wealth of staggering proportions in fewer and fewer hands, which means that for every big winner, there are, literally, tens of thousands of losers. We're seeing the drastic reduction in unionization that once brought many working men (in the United States, particularly white men) many benefits. We're seeing the reduction of social services. Many men who once looked forward to lives with decently paying and secure middle-class jobs simply can't look forward to that any longer. I say to them, sure, do something about this, but just don't blame women (or immigrants or racialized minorities).

If we're trying to accelerate the advancement of women, in certain fields or certain companies men might well lose out more than half the time for a while. If men hold most corporate middle and senior management positions, and if we want the composition of those positions to look more like their workforce and customers—not only to be part of a more equitable society but also in order to function more successfully—then it does mean that we need to hire or promote more women than men until things begin to even out. Let's be honest about that. Men can take it.

Despite impressive progress in the direction of gender equality over the past decades, the deck is still stacked against women in the world of work. This is doubly true for women of color who face even stronger hurdles and biases. At the very top, women in the United States overall account for only 19 percent of so-called C-suite positions (chief executive officer, chief financial officer, etc.) while women of color (who as a group, represent about 20 percent of the population), hold only 3 percent of such positions.[9]

Indeed, one place where the deck has been particularly stacked is in the hiring and advancement of women up the corporate ladder. This has received more attention in recent years, in part because of the efforts of organizations such as Catalyst and Lean In.

I spoke to one woman vice president from a global asset management company linked to an insurance megacompany. Catherine said her company had made a commitment to gender equality and the advancement of women, but they were barely making progress. "We were hiring equally at the entry level, but as we went up to higher grades, numbers dropped off." When they dug more deeply, "we found that women weren't leaving at a higher percentage, but were getting stuck in the murky middle." We often think of the glass ceiling as being way up the corporate ladder, but Catherine says they discovered the glass ceiling was right there at the middle.

What is the impact of the barriers to promotion and to women's career advancement? The numbers tell it all. As you go up the corporate hierarchy, you're going to find vastly more men at the top.

THE INCREDIBLE SHRINKING WOMAN

	Women	Men
	% of positions held	% of positions held
Entry level	46	54
Manager	37	63
Senior manager/ director	33	67
Vice president	29	71
Senior vice president	24	76
C-Suite	19	81

US data from McKinsey & Company, Lean In,
Women in the Workplace 2016

Although a lot of talk these days in corporate circles is about the paucity of women in the more exalted positions and on corporate boards, by sheer numbers alone, the bigger concern is down the pecking order.

We're missing a lot of women.

Even going up one level from entry level to manager, we're missing millions and millions of women who should be there.

Women face profound, multiple, and divergent barriers. Not only are there barriers from floor to floor, but even walking across your office or shop floor can smack you into another wall. Even if the barriers might be invisible to many men, women are acutely and painfully aware of them. And some barriers work only on certain groups of women—the young or old, the single woman or pregnant, the lesbian, the black, Asian, or Hispanic, the Muslim, the physically challenged—and many of those same barriers work on certain groups of men.

Here are some of the barriers women face:

Women's abilities devalued. A group of researchers did a test with professors who ran labs in biology, chemistry, and physics. The researchers wrote up a single resume pretending it was for a graduating student applying for a laboratory management position. In half the submissions, the researchers gave the student a female name, in the other half a male name, but it was the exact same resume. The hiring professors said they'd pay the "female" 14 percent less ($26,500 versus $30,200) than the "male." They said the "female" was less hireable than the "male." And they offered fewer mentoring opportunities. It didn't matter how old the hiring professor was or even whether they were a male or female themselves.[10] Simply put, women's abilities were devalued. Put a man and a woman with equal abilities and an equal resume side by side, and the man gets the job, gets the mentorship, gets the higher pay.

Exclusion from the club. Informal ties built up in comfortable moments over a coffee or a drink, watching a game, or a dinner with the family can have a nice impact when it comes to hiring and advancement. We want to work with people we feel comfortable with, and we want to hire people we trust at a personal level.

That's fine, but women are often excluded from these informal networks. It wouldn't even occur to some men to include a woman colleague in mentoring or after-work events. Some industries traditionally chose environments for social events that were hostile to women: I spoke to a man in a mining company (before he left in disgust) that regularly took clients to strip clubs. In other cases, there are men who worry about mentoring a woman or hanging out socially. Will coworkers suspect they're having an affair? What will he tell his wife? Will there be more rumors if the woman gets a promotion?

It turns out that not only men have these concerns. A *New York Times*/Morning Consult poll asked both women and men whether they felt it was appropriate for them to have one-on-one contact with someone of the other sex who was not your spouse. Grab a bite to eat at lunchtime? Only 43 percent of women and 52 percent of men said it was appropriate. Drive in a car together? That's okay only to 47 and 58 percent. Even having a work meeting was a no-no for many: one-third of both women and men thought it inappropriate or they weren't sure.[11]

Perhaps part of women's responses was implicitly answering a slightly different question; that is, not whether it was appropriate per se but simply whether they'd be worried about possible sexual harassment. But the similarity of responses to the workplace meeting question suggests that many women felt the same as men: they feared misperceptions by workmates, friends, or a spouse, feared sending out the wrong messages, and held the same tired old assumption that women and men should inhabit separate spheres, whether going to the restroom or hanging out. The fact that women's and men's responses were similar shows that gender relations and gender inequality are part of a system that, while disproportionately benefiting men, many women have bought into and perpetuated as well.

Language, not eyes, are the mirror to our souls. Numerous studies and the accounts of many women show we use a different vocabulary to describe women in the workplace.

The vocabulary reflects sexist bias. As multiple academic studies have shown, and as Lean In and McKinsey & Company note in their *Women in the Workplace* report, "If a woman is competent, she does not seem nice enough, but if she seems nice, she is considered less competent. This bias often surfaces in the way women are described, both in passing and in performance reviews. When a woman asserts herself, she is often called 'aggressive,' 'ambitious,' or 'out for herself.' When a man does the same, he is seen as 'confident' and 'strong.'"[12]

Words carry meaning, which is why we have them. Meaning creates impact. And so, women get dropped into a double bind: play the game as men have defined it and pay a price; don't play the game and pay a price.

Women still viewed first as mothers. One woman, Angela, tells me this story: "I am the only woman in a boardroom full of men and at the beginning of the meeting someone says to me, 'So what's your background besides being a mom?'"

Perhaps we can write that off as friendly chitchat, and I'm guessing the man thought he was making her feel comfortable. But to Angela it felt like a diminution of why she was at the table—that is, not as a mom, but because of her professional qualifications. The problem is that it isn't a one-off. Assumptions about women's family priorities versus men's are rampant in workplaces and hold women back. One man I spoke to said his company was hiring for a position, and the candidates were narrowed down to a thirtyish man or a thirtyish woman. The company wasn't allowed to ask questions about either's plans to have children or even family status, although the male candidate had slipped in a comment about how supportive his wife was. (Code words for "I am straight," "I'm settled and dependable," and "She won't raise a fuss when I check work email during dinner.") The hiring committee decided that chances were good that the woman would be having a baby in the next four or five years. Not only would she be taking maternity leave, but her family responsibilities afterward would keep her from prioritizing work. They didn't say the same thing about the man, although there was exactly the same chance that he'd have a child, and in his generation more and more men are taking parental leave and prioritizing family over work. They hired the man.

Making assumptions about women: Darisha tells me: "I kept getting passed over for travel to meet clients. Finally I asked my supervisor why I was never considered. The supervisor looked surprised. 'Oh, I just assumed you wouldn't be able to go because you've got young kids.'" She replied that so did some of the men who were traveling. It doesn't matter that the supervisor was well-meaning. The impact of his actions was to exclude Darisha from career-advancing activities.

Lack of family-friendly policies. Although we shouldn't assume women will be getting pregnant or have more family responsibilities than men, if we want workplaces that equally include and promote women, we must recognize that in the average home, women are still doing more child rearing and housework than men. One woman says, "They always did the departmental meeting on Monday mornings at eight thirty. Sometimes I made it on time, but normally I was taking the kids to school." People said they understood, but there was no way she could contribute the same as others. This type of thing is only the tip of the iceberg. Most workplaces still lack flexible hours, and most workers, at least in the United States, have only minimal, unpaid parental leave. Although these deficits disproportionately affect women, more and more men are stung by the lack of family-friendly policies and programs. Even where there are flex hours and leave, women and men are reticent to take advantage for fear of how it will affect their careers.[13]

The impact of domestic violence. Women disproportionately experience relationship violence that causes physical injury. The result is long nights lived in fear (and hence a reduced ability to function optimally at work), arriving late because a husband hid the car keys, or missing work altogether because she is at the hospital or has an embarrassing bruise. Sadly, few employers have specific policies to support employees experiencing domestic violence, and managers are rarely trained to spot the signs of violence and be supportive.[14]

Adding all this together, the impact is massive. A law came into effect in England in 2018 that requires companies to report the female/male pay gap. This law is worded to prevent companies from spinning the facts to mask what's going on, something that has happened in the United States where, for example, Adobe, Expedia, and Mastercard have apparently reported a 0 percentage pay gap, whereas their UK counterparts report, respectively, 18.2, 17.9, and 19.8 percent gaps. The figures coming out as a result of this law are startling: in the UK's largest bank, HSBC, the average woman makes 59 percent less than men, reflecting that women tend to be in lower-paying and junior roles. At Goldman Sachs, it's 55 percent; Barclays, 48 percent; and Deloitte, 43 percent. In the oil, gas, and manufacturing industries, it's closer to the UK national average, with a 23 percent gap at BP and 14 percent at 3M—better but still far from equal.[15]

In response to growing concern but sluggish progress worldwide, Iceland has taken the dramatic step in announcing it will be legally enforcing equal pay. The law affects all public and private companies with more than twenty-five employees. Large firms had one year (until the end of 2018) to comply. Small firms have four years to get it right (until the end of 2022). Sooner or later, they all must independently certify they are paying equally for work of equal value—and if they aren't, they will face daily fines. Of course that doesn't in itself address job ghettoes for women. But now some Icelandic companies are taking action. Over the past few years, Reykjavik Energy, the country's premier provider of power, raised the percentage of women managers from 29 to 49 percent while at the same time working to adjust any existing pay gaps. Now there still is a gap—0.2 percent on the women's side.[16]

Even in male-dominated industries, change can be rapid and dramatic.

We're finally seeing lots of talk and some action on equal pay and hiring and promotion of women by some employers: new mentoring programs, support circles for women or for men who want to support gender equality in the workplace. But action is slow and remains piecemeal, pretty much dependent on the commitment of a particular employer. The fact is, although some companies will act either because they know it's the right thing to do or because they can make a strong economic argument, for the economy to shift as a whole, we need strong government action. And for action in either individual companies or at the governmental level, we need men to strongly count themselves in.

The Poisoned Workplace and Sexual Harassment

Picture the scene: A work meeting. One man, the friendly jokester of the department, comes out with a blatantly sexist comment meant as a joke. Some men and one woman laugh, but the eyes of many men and women shoot down onto their notes. Faced with this scene, we often ask the wrong question: how should the women react? In part, it's the wrong question because, too often, if a woman raises an objection, she's seen as humorless or uptight. In effect she's blamed for creating the problem.

The main reason it's the wrong question, though, is because the first question we should be asking is, what should the *men* do? (It's exactly the same issue as expecting LGBTQ folks to be the ones responding to homophobia; black, Asian, or Latino people to racism; Muslims or Jews to challenge anti-Islamic or anti-Semitic comments.)

Many men feel uncomfortable about the actions of some male coworkers but they choose to stay silent. Perhaps our silence is because we don't understand the grinding impact these words and actions have. Perhaps the inappropriate behavior originates from a workplace superior and it's often just as difficult for men to confront that person. But even when it's a coworker and we know we should speak out, what keeps men silent? Remember my discussion in chapter 3 about the paradox of men's power? Men unconsciously worry that we should be seen as one of the boys.

It would be easy to imagine, especially in the wake of

the revelations pouring out of Hollywood and beyond, that when we talk about sexual harassment we're talking chiefly about sexual assault or actions bordering on assault. These egregious things absolutely do happen (and are part of the subject of a separate chapter). But when men listen to women, we quickly discover that for many women, indeed a majority of women, the thing that presses on them in the most frequent ways are unwanted remarks about their bodies, demeaning comments, unwanted touch, and so forth. It's the joke on the shop floor that demeans women, the manager or coworker who figures his job description includes giving little shoulder rubs to women, the guy who persistently asks women out for dates, the coworker or manager who every morning tells a woman how good she looks.

It's not like this happens once in a lifetime. When we men listen, women will tell us it's like the drip, drip, drip of a tap that keeps you awake at night. It's the background hum in too many workplaces, and for some women, it's the thing that you know awaits you each and every day.

Sure, women develop strategies. They try to avoid working with certain men, they requests transfers, they leave their jobs. Faced with jokes and comments, as Angela told me, "Over the years we learn to navigate these situations either by calling them out, through humor, wit, or playing stupid."

But why should the onus be on women? Why should they be the ones cleaning up a workplace mess created by some men? The answer is simple: they should not.

Extensive and Harmful

A careful study by the US Equal Employment Opportunity Commission gives us a snapshot of the extent of sexual harassment in the workplace. And it also highlights the importance of what questions men must ask if we want to understand the problem.

Researchers asked women if they'd ever experienced sexual harassment in the workplace. A large number, 25 percent of women, said yes. That would be one in four of the women you've ever worked with.

But that question left the definition of sexual harassment up to the responder. She might have thought it only meant sexual coercion or assault or she might have included other forms of harassment. When researchers made the question more specific and asked women if they'd ever experienced "unwanted sexual attention or sexual coercion," the number shot up to an even larger 40 percent.

It gets worse. The researchers then included behaviors that they termed *gender harassment* but which many, myself included, normally include under the blanket term *sexual harassment*. This includes sexist and demeaning name-calling, anti-female jokes, displaying pornography, and so on. When they asked about these things, 60 percent of women said they've experienced such things at work.[17] (This is about the same number of LGBTQ respondents who report experiencing derogatory comments about sexual orientation and gender identity. Add on harassment based on race, age, religion, and disability, and you start seeing how extensive the harassment problem is.)

What's the result of this, both the most egregious forms of workplace abuse we're hearing so much about and the drip, drip, drip of things someone might think are more innocuous? Harassment can make someone nervous and fearful when they have to work with a certain person—and thus they become less productive. It can make someone who complains fear for her job. It can cause worries about personal safety—I've talked to police officers and soldiers (both female and male) about being in danger because they're with someone they no longer trust.

Harassment can blast its poison into a whole workplace. It can cause suspicion and distrust and fuel rumors. It can be enormously expensive, from lost work time during a complaints process to absenteeism to having to replace staff who quit to the huge cost of formal investigations and settlements.

It can lead to a drop in public confidence. Just look at the fallout from a growing and appallingly long list of complaints about sexual harassment in the corporate world. For example, when reports came out of predatory sexual behavior by Uber's founder, thousands and thousands of people stopped using the service.

Sexual harassment is a key workplace barrier to gender equality because it reinforces workplace cultures where women are constantly belittled. And because harassment can often be committed by those with more power in the workplace, and such people are disproportionately men, women have often been stymied to stop it. Yes, men can experience sexual harassment at work. But even then, it's disproportionately committed by men, not only because they're more likely to be in positions of power, but because part of the collective privilege men have enjoyed is to control the public and work space.

The Complicated Nature of Workplace Harassment

There's a lot of misunderstanding about workplace sexual harassment. Yes, it can include sexual assault or explicitly sexist slurs (just like workplace harassment can include explicitly racist or homophobic slurs). More and more men understand the problem with that—and the vast majority would neither commit nor condone sexual assault. What confuses many men are the more subtle factors that create that drip, drip, drip I was speaking about. Let me give you some examples.

Casual physical contact: I give a coworker a friendly pat on the shoulder. For most of us, an occasional and friendly touch wouldn't be experienced as harassing. But what if I pat a coworker on the butt? Probably fine if my coworker is a fellow linebacker on the Green Bay Packers; not so cool if she or he is the accountant in the next office. What if my shoulder pat becomes a mini-backrub? What if that pat lingers or happens several times a day?

All this is culturally bound. Go to Barcelona or Rio de Janeiro and everyone, men and women, women and women,

men and men, seem to be kissing each other on the cheek, even at work. At the other extreme, step into an office with very orthodox Muslims or Jews, and men and women won't even shake hands.

Jokes: I don't think there is a culture that doesn't tell jokes. But what about jokes with a sexual theme? And who's to say what joke is appropriate or not?

Frequency: A colleague or my admin assistant comes back from a two-week holiday in Jamaica. I say, "You're looking great." She (or he) might welcome the compliment. But what if I start off each day commenting about how great she looks?

Reporting relationship: I'm a friendly guy. I like complimenting people. So I tell a woman at work I like how she's done her hair. I might give her a friendly hug. I make sure I'll sit with her during a break now and then. I'll ask about her weekend. If we're friends outside of work, these things might be fine. But if we're only work friends, maybe not. That's even truer if I'm her (or his) boss. That would make it really hard for her to tell me this attention makes her feel uncomfortable.

Where it happens: I have a good friend at work. We tease each other about our looks and our sex lives. That's probably cool. But it changes if I start saying these things at a department meeting or in front of others.

Tone of voice, choice of words, and body language: My co-worker mentions she's going clothes shopping after work. The next morning she comes in wearing a new sweater. I could say, "That looks great on you." Probably just fine. But instead I say, "Man, you look hot in that," and I stare at her breasts. You can see the problem.

Flirting and asking out: I ask a coworker out on a date. She (or he) says, "I'm kind of busy." That might mean "no," but it might mean she's, well, kind of busy. I wait a couple of weeks and ask again. Another excuse. Years of high school training should have prepared me for this moment. She is saying no and is trying to let me down nicely. And if I keep asking, it will be the same as continuing to pester her (or him) just as if she had clearly said "no" from the start.

Whatever it is, I've heard men say, "I meant that as a compliment" or "I was joking." The thing is, a compliment or a joke should make someone feel good. Embarrassed? Uncomfortable? Scared? It's obviously not working.

It's difficult new terrain that men and women must negotiate when it comes to potential harassment. When a man says, "I didn't intend to offend anyone," it takes us to the heart of what harassment is and isn't. The key is usually not a person's intention, but rather the impact of their words or actions. (The obvious exceptions—and these always constitute harassment—are implicit or explicit offers of favors in exchange for sex, or aggressive behaviors that are meant to hurt, embarrass, or intimidate.)

Once we look at it from the point of view of impact, we start being able to sort out appropriate from inappropriate workplace behavior. We start understanding that many forms of sexual harassment aren't an absolute you can carve onto a new set of Ten Commandments. I've seen company policies that, in addition to being legalistic wordplay, simply aren't based on the reality that harassment often depends on the context, on people's work and personal relationships, and on impact.

Yet, is harassment arbitrary or about too-easily bruised feelings? Say I'm a vegetarian and you eat a chicken sandwich at the next desk over. Can I claim that you're harassing me? Although harassment is about impact, it isn't arbitrary. For my complaint to be successful, it must be something that a reasonable person might feel.

All this complexity points to the need for serious and thoughtful responses in our workplaces. After all, the US Equal Employment Opportunity Commission reports that "three out of four individuals who experienced harassment never even talked to a supervisor, manager, or union representative about the harassing conduct." Why not? "Because they fear disbelief of their claim, inaction on their claim, blame, or social or professional retaliation."[18]

In most cases women and men who experience any form of workplace harassment, including a poisoned work environment, don't want retribution or a financial payout, unless the experience is particularly severe or damaging. They simply want that inappropriate and hurtful behavior to stop. Having a workplace policy simply isn't enough. What we also need is to give men and women the knowledge and practical tools to speak out, to say something to their friends or workmates. We need managers, who are still disproportionately men as you go up the ladder, to understand the urgency of the problem, but to also have the practical tools to respond in an effective, fair, and educational way.

My own approach, which I've brought into a number of government agencies, companies, and parts of the United Nations, is one that focuses on the impact and nuances of workplace harassment and gives managers tools to stop it. I called it Red Light, Green Light, and for readers who'd like to get some practical tips, I invite you to check out appendix 3 (page 237).

A Final Confusion for Men About Workplace Harassment

With a laugh, the man says, "She complained that guys hit on her. Man, I'd love it if women gave me attention like that."

Here we're back to issues around the invisibility of privilege discussed in chapter 2. Sure, we might enjoy compliments on our appearance. But in a world of unequal power and privilege, a compliment becomes something different. First of all, men enjoy the privilege that they are far less likely to have been sexually assaulted, especially by a woman. (Although boys do experience sexual assault more often than we once thought—and as with girls, most often by a family member, coach, religious official, or close family acquaintance . . . that is, someone in a position of trust and accessibility—it is still less common than what girls experience.)

I and others who speak on university campuses have asked this question to the men in the audience: Raise your hand if you've ever given clear instructions to a friend or roommate when you're going out with someone for a first time, or asked a friend to watch your drink for fear of being drugged, or thought twice about walking to the library at night for fear of violence, or had to push someone away who was groping at you, or been scared because you were followed on the street by someone making comments about how good you looked? A straggle of hands go up. Then when we ask the women present? Every woman's hand shoots toward the ceiling.[19]

That's the background, the life experience that goes into daily encounters, whether a wolf whistle or comment on the street, or that unwanted touch or comment at work.

Furthermore, men historically have had the privilege of not being valued first for our looks and our bodies. So we don't bring worries into the workplace about being there as equals.

Similarly, we don't live in a society where men have been systematically demeaned and degraded by women. So when I hear a woman repeat an anti-male joke or stereotype (say about men's inability to look after a baby, or talk about feelings, or do housework) I will definitely feel annoyed, but I won't feel demeaned or threatened or attacked. I know that these stereotypes do many men a disservice, but also know they aren't used as a weapon for women to systematically oppress us.

These comments on privilege have long been understood by some men, such as gay men who've endured homophobia or men of color who've endured racism. For them a casual "joke" or comment carries with it not only a lifetime but centuries of hatred and oppression, discrimination and fear.

All this underscores why we need to worry about the impact of certain words and behavior.

Which takes us back to the point that most workplace sexual harassment is about impact and not intent. The impact is conditioned by a whole society of gender inequality, the sexual objectification of women, and sexual violence against women. We get rid of those things, and we have better and more relaxed workplaces, where gender equality proves beneficial for women and for men.

That's why we need men to make a commitment to gender-equitable workplaces free of harassment. We need solid policies but also smart and reoccurring training of staff and managers to prevent or respond promptly to harassment, and we need to hold managers accountable.

Family-Friendlier Workplaces

Let me quickly mention one final workplace issue. The benefits of gender equality will be clearly felt by both women *and* men as we create workplaces that recognize we have lives outside of our jobs.

The first big demands for work-life balance came as women entered certain professions such as law in ever-greater numbers. They found an environment that demanded long hours and that rewarded those who could master a winner-take-all mentality whatever the personal cost. It was one thing to do this as a new graduate, but sustaining that in order to become a partner was extremely difficult if you also wanted to prioritize your family. Women voted with their feet and in large numbers left the big firms and pursued careers as in-house corporate or government lawyers. Or they left law altogether.

Similar concerns have emerged not only in all the professions, but throughout the workforce.

Women have pushed for changes and in many cases have been successful. They've won flexible work time (so that they could take or pick up children at school or simply avoid the idiotic jams on the road or public transit at rush hour). Some jobs now allow for telecommuting and working from home, although there are costs and benefits of doing so. Women have won family leave to care for sick family members. They've pushed for meetings to avoid early mornings or late afternoons. And, in the United States, the one developed country without federally mandated and paid-for parental leave, they've won parental leave in some companies and in government workplaces.

A growing number of men are embracing these changes, especially as more men are taking on an active and central role as parents.

It's not only the lack of such policies that presents a barrier to women's employment and advancement. If such policies exist but our employers don't actively promote them, we have a problem. Many women and men don't take advantage of flexible workplace policies for the simple reason that they assume it would be frowned upon and a sign of a lack of ambition.

That's why leadership is so important. And since men are still disproportionately the ones in leadership positions, it means men have a disproportionate role to play.

That's why I enjoyed meeting a British banker, a senior VP based in Singapore. "I'm seeing a growing trend," he said, "of men demanding to spend more time with children, especially at the early stage. This coincides [fortuitously] with women wanting to pursue their own careers."

Although these changes are happening, he notes that traditional roles still have a strong hold in the corporate world. "We must provide a dynamic environment for staff to pursue work-life balance."

What does that mean in his case?

The answer is leadership by example. And it's leadership that clearly expresses what he wants in his life. He says, "I make pancakes for my children each morning. I arrive at work after nine." Definitely not banker's hours.

Does that hurt his work or his own prospects? "I feel I've become a far better leader and business professional because I've learned from my children and from the ways they call me out."

This begins to point to the biggest change in men's lives brought about by the push for gender equality. The single biggest way men will contribute to gender equality and the single most important and positive change that men are enjoying.

I call it the Dad Shift.

5

THE DAD SHIFT

The Gender Equality Advantage of Fatherhood

n one minute, Liam will be reborn as a father.

It will be the most extraordinary moment of his life since he himself squirmed his way onto the planet thirty-three years before.

We think that the role of fathers is pretty fixed by nature—you know, woman the nurturer, man the hunter. But as Liam is about to discover, his role will be determined by the attitudes of those around him, the social supports, and the choices that both he and his wife make.

He would be overwhelmed if he were thinking—which as the seconds count down he definitely is not—about how the choices he and his wife, Lisa, make will have profound implications not only for them and their child, but also as part of a society redefining fatherhood, a pivotal moment for gender equality and positive changes in men's lives for decades and centuries to come.

Normally we think of the moment a child comes into the world as the birth of one person. But, in fact, it is also the birth of mothers and fathers.

That moment is, indeed, momentous. It's much more than a new label. Becoming a father (either biologically or by adopting or even forming a close nurturing bond with a grandchild, nephew, niece, or family friend) means you've just established a link to the future of humanity.

And with that link comes the potential for men's greatest contribution to gender equality.[1]

Beyond the Busted Images of Fatherhood

Until fairly recently, our world had a few wildly contrasting images of fatherhood.

There was *Father Knows Best*. Fathers are wise and patient. Basic idea: Fathers are the perfect center of a perfect family universe.

And then there's Homer Simpson—dolt extraordinaire, thoughtless and inept. Basic idea: Men really aren't capable as parents.

There's a third image captured in that most threatening of sentences, "Wait till your father comes home." Dad is the punisher and ultimate disciplinarian. Basic idea: A father is policeman, God, and executioner all rolled into one.

And let's throw in one more image. The good dad who "helps out." It's not his real job, but he pitches in and does his best to squeeze in some quality time with the kids. Ba-

sic idea: Dads are good to have around, sort of like a relief
pitcher ready to take the mound in a moment of need.

These ideas didn't spring from out of the blue, but they're
hopelessly at odds with the emerging realities of fathers. After all, over the past three decades, US fathers have increased
the amount of time they spend with children on workdays by
a whopping 65 percent.[2]

This change is happening around the world. Over the
past decade, I haven't visited a single country on any continent where I don't meet men who are busy transforming
what it means to be a dad, although some places certainly
have come much further along than others.

In 1977, 64 percent of US men thought it best if a man
earns money and women take care of home and children.
By 2008, this had dropped to 39 percent.[3]

According to a 2016 study we've done at Promundo, half
of US fathers said they either equally share caregiving or are
their child's primary caregiver. And although their female
partners have a different take (only 34 percent say their male
partner does equal or primary caregiving), even this lower
figure is a big improvement from their fathers' generation.[4]

In 1970, there were six men in the United States who
identified themselves as stay-at-home dads. (That's not a
typo. Yes, six.) By 2012, the number had skyrocketed to two
million.[5] The state with the highest proportion of stay-at-
home dads is South Dakota (39 percent of stay-at-home parents), followed by West Virginia.

Men have been ramping up the amount of housework

we do and (this is significant) taking responsibility for it rather than just picking up the broom when a wife or girl-friend tells us to. Between the mid-1960s and the start of the twenty-first century, men's contribution to housework doubled, from 15 to 30 percent of the total. This, plus the spread of labor-saving devices and women working longer hours outside the home, meant that women were spending two hours less a week on housework.[6]

The changes since the rise of modern feminism are dramatic:

- The hours that US fathers spend doing child-care jumped from 2.5 in 1965 to 7 hours per week in 2011, and housework from 4 to 10 hours per week. Meanwhile, mothers' time do-ing childcare has also increased, from 10 to 14 hours, while housework has decreased from 32 to 18 hours.[7]
- Between 1965 and 2000, married fathers in the United States doubled the time they were spending exclusively on childcare (meaning not counting sticking the kid in the car with you to do an errand or watching TV together).[8] Ac-cording to another US study, men's time con-tribution to childcare tripled between 1965 and 2003.[9]
- In the United Kingdom, between 1975 and 1997, care by dads for infants and the young rose by eight times, from a pathetic 15 minutes to 2 hours

on the average working day.[10] In just three years, between 2002 and 2005, the percentage of new fathers in the United Kingdom working flexible hours so they could spend more time with their infants jumped mightily from 11 percent to 31 percent.[11]

• And while barely over half (57 percent) of Canadian fathers with preschoolers reported daily participation in childcare in 1986, twenty years later, in 2005, it was 73 percent. It was a big increase, although still lagging behind the 90 percent of moms who were doing the same.[12]

Lest we get giddy about these changes, let's acknowledge we still have a long way to go. Yes, there are homes where housework and parenting duties are equally shared between a mother and a father. There are some homes where men are doing more work in the home than a female partner; there are some stay-at-home dads. There are single-father households. There are two-dad households as more gay fathers either adopt or live with the biological children of one of the men.

But when it comes to equality of work in the home, across society as a whole, women still do more of the housework and childcare. And even though women on average do less hours of paid work then men, in most of the world, women spend more total hours working in paid and unpaid work combined.

- In the United States, the average guy does a total of 7.9 hours of work a day (2.5 unpaid and 5.4 hours paid). Women do 8.1 hours, split fifty-fifty between paid and unpaid work.
- In Canada, men total 8.4 hours of work per day (2.7 unpaid and 5.7 paid). For women, it's 8.8 (4.2 unpaid and 4.5 paid—the figures have been rounded out).
- The United Kingdom sees men doing 7.3 hours of work per day (2.3 unpaid and 5.0 paid), while women do 7.6 hours (4.3 unpaid and 3.3 paid).
- Sweden (along with the other Nordic countries) has the lowest gap, although it is still significant: For men, it's 2.6 hours unpaid and 5.4 hours paid work. For women, it's 3.4 hours unpaid and 4.5 hours paid.
- Some countries are off the charts: In Japan, there is a massive gap both in unpaid and paid work: Men do only 1 hour of unpaid work a day compared to women's 5 hours a day. And 7.9 hours of paid work versus 3.4 for women.[13]

Another study, using different categories, compares the hours men and women spend in caring for household members. In the United States, men spend 19 minutes per day compared to women's 41 minutes. In Canada it's 21 minutes for men compared to 44 minutes for women. In the United Kingdom, 34 compared to 62 minutes.[14]

While antiquated ideas about fatherhood might be

hopelessly out of date, long-established norms live on as a barrier to the gender-equitable role that a renewed fatherhood can play. Getting rid of these norms, however, isn't easy because they live on not simply in our heads but in the ways we have set up our society, in particular the world of work. After all, there are a lot of fathers who'd like to play an equal or at least a much bigger role, and many mothers who would enthusiastically agree. True, many men haven't had a chance to learn parenting skills. But more than that, they don't have the social support, paid leave, and company encouragement that is essential. We need to discover both the tools that individual men need and the policy directions we all need to more quickly and definitively create a world where men are doing one-half of the care work. As we'll see, this will be good for women, good for children, and good for men ourselves. And more than any other single factor, it will be critical for achieving gender equality.

Beyond that, I would argue this: The transformation of fatherhood will be, for men, what feminism has been for women. It is the thing that is redefining our lives in a powerful, life-affirming, forward-moving way.

However, for this transformation to take place, we need concerted action by men and women working together to redefine fatherhood, and to make sure there is the social framework to do so.

But is the idea of transforming fatherhood wishful thinking? For one thing, are we working against biology and all of human history?

Evolution and Hormones

In 1879 a Swiss zoologist named Hermann Fol first observed the fertilization of an egg by a sperm cell. As strange as it now seems, until then no one knew for certain that it took only one sperm cell to carry out this momentous task. No one had ever proven that every child has only a single biological father.

As with many things having to do with the traditional roles of women and men, there is some obvious biology involved. A biological mother forms an extraordinary physical and emotional bond with the child who lives within her body, hears her heartbeat, and senses her energy and emotions for nine months. There is also the equally extraordinary physical and emotional bond developed during breastfeeding.

But what about the woman who adopts or who doesn't breastfeed? We still ascribe to her a biological ability that we've often assumed a man is lacking. We often justify men's secondary role in traditional parenting (and a very distant second at that) as being about biology.

So let's look for a second at the biology of fatherhood.

Humans are part of a small minority of mammals where fathers give direct care to the young—only about 10 percent of 5,400 mammal species. Among primates, though, 40 percent do, but that's mainly monkeys. None of the other great apes—chimpanzees, gorillas, bonobos, and orangutans—have caregiving fathers. Other great ape mothers usually don't trust anyone else, female or male, to hold their babies.[15]

What in our evolutionary history set early hominins on a different parenting path around two million years ago?

I put that question to evolutionary biologist Sarah Blaffer Hrdy, professor emeritus at the University of California–Davis. She answers that cooperative parenting (that is, having males and other females share some responsibility with mothers) was the key to our subsequent evolution. This evolution includes the development of much bigger brains, increase in female body size relative to males, prolonged childhood, and extended lifespans.

But it's one thing to say that human evolution has created the possibility of hands-on fathers. However, doesn't a woman's hormonal mix set her up for parenting in a way that a man will never enjoy?

It's true that males don't get the staggering boost of prolactin and oxytocin that is released in women during labor or after stimulation of her nipples. But amazing research is now showing that males in close contact with either pregnant mothers or newborn babies have increased levels of prolactin. Even fifteen minutes of holding a baby produces this effect.[16] And the result? For one thing, as with the mother, this leads to a heightened response to the needs of a baby when they hear the baby cry.

Meanwhile, fathers have significant declines in their testosterone and estradiol levels before their baby is born.[17]

Perhaps the most telling point is that these hormonal changes in males aren't a one-time activity. The more a man is an involved caregiver, the more he has these hormonal effects. For example, when exposed to a crying infant, experienced fathers show a bigger boost in prolactin compared to first-time fathers.[18]

Thus active parenting for men produces fathers who are more hormonally primed to be even more active. In other words, there's a positive feedback loop—the more you do it, the more you're biologically priming yourself to do it. But it's not simply that these hormonal changes cause nurturing behavior. Rather, a dad's activities combined with his past experiences lead to hormonal shifts that make him more sensitive to the needs of infants. This sensitivity leads to more activity that fortifies these hormonal changes.

Although the hormonal shifts aren't as dramatic as in females, this much is clear: human males have evolved to be caregivers.

When Dads Dropped the Ball

Tribal societies—those embodiments of the long journey of humanity—show great diversity in the role of fathers. In the Central African Republic, Aka fathers (the so-called pygmies) are the world leaders for looking after kids. In a twenty-four-hour day, they are either holding or within arm's length or eyesight of their children 88 percent of the time. At the other end of the spectrum, Kipsigis fathers in Kenya never hold an infant during the first year. Not once.[19]

There is a pattern that seems to have determined which societies have a higher or lower participation of fathers. This pattern is key for understanding the role of male caregivers in promoting, or thwarting, gender quality.

I talked earlier about the emergence of patriarchal societies around eight or ten thousand years ago. Humans were putting down greater roots and moving from foraging for subsistence to domesticating animals and plants. The earlier foraging (hunter-gatherer) societies tended to be societies based on a high (or at least higher) level of gender equality. In these, men did more caring of infants and children. But domesticating animals and cultivating plants were part of a process of social change that often included women moving away to live with a male partner's family. These societies tended to be more patriarchal. The reason men assumed increasing power over women (including women's reproduction) was probably because through such control men could ensure their animals and land could be passed on to their offspring. That's why, if you pick up the Old Testament, the Hebrew Torah, and flip to the book of Numbers, you'll see many laws about inheritance, usually to the male child. This was a big deal in all the societies in that region in the years that patriarchy was evolving and getting codified in law. And within these societies, men tended to do less caregiving of the young.

Benefits of the New Fatherhood

Although men may have evolved to have the capacity to be active caregivers, many men (and in some cultures, most men) haven't chosen to do so. In a moment, we'll look at steps we can take to transform fatherhood. But that begs the question: why bother trying to promote change if it isn't going to do much good for anyone? Or to put it differently, why is it absolutely imperative that we move steadily and forcefully toward a world where men are doing one-half of the caregiving work?

The answer was obvious to one woman I interviewed. With her son now grown up, Andrea spoke of the life plans she abandoned because almost all the caregiving work fell on her shoulders. "I watched dreams get put out with the garbage. And after a while I no longer had the energy to dream those dreams, to strive anymore. That's the crappy part, because somewhere underneath was a strong person."

And then there is Jen, who tried to pursue her dreams, even completing a master's in social work. But when her second child came, she dropped out of the workforce. When her kids were well into their teens, she returned to work outside the home. It surprised her how difficult it was to find a job with a thin resume. The drop in income associated with starting again at the ground level was not as difficult as the toll on her self-esteem. "I never had any doubts professionally. [But] coming back, even now, I question myself all the time. Some little mistake at work and I'll kill myself for it."

Mothers take a huge economic hit for having children. Not only do they take off more time to look after babies and young children, but they also, more so than men, disproportionately take limiting jobs and make limiting career decisions because of domestic responsibilities. They're more likely to work part-time or in less ambitious jobs because they have disproportionate responsibility for taking the kids to doctors' appointments and after-school lessons or for staying home when a child is sick. And even if they aren't taking more time, employers will often *perceive* that their role as mothers will get in the way of their job.

Economists Barth, Kerr, Olivetti, and Goldin pick apart US census data from 2000 to demonstrate convincingly that the major factor in women's lower earning is the household division of labor—that is, women's greater responsibility as mothers.[20]

And as both Andrea and Jen show, women also take a huge emotional hit. For one thing, there is a perception about women's value. As a society that places the most value on earning money and on leadership outside the home, we've devalued the many practical, intellectual, educational, and emotional skills required to be a good parent and to manage a house.

The impact of women's disproportionate responsibility for childcare goes well beyond the world of work. It affects, for example, women's participation in political life. Again, this is partly about perception of women's abilities, but it's also about time. One study showed the relationship between women's societal power and close father-child relations. In tribal cultures with high or moderate female participation in public decision making, 72 percent had close father-child relations. But in those where females were excluded from public decision making, only 21 percent had close father-child relations.[21]

What all this means is that women stand to benefit

tremendously when men take on their share of parenting and domestic tasks. It will free up extra hours women can devote to advancing in their education and careers. It will mean that more men will enter traditionally "women's" jobs and vice versa, which will give more impetus to equal pay. It will mean that a mother or mother-to-be won't be seen as a workplace problem (compared to a man) but will be seen as a normal worker at that stage of life.

Men's greater participation in parenting and housework also leads to improvements in women's health. According to various international studies, when men are involved from the start in prenatal visits to the doctor and when they are present during delivery, women experience safer, shorter, and less painful births.[22] Male involvement supporting a female partner during pregnancy and following birth reduces the odds of postpartum depression and increases women's utilization of health services.[23] Breastfeeding mothers who are supported by their partners have fewer breastfeeding problems and are more likely to continue with full breast-feeding at six months.[24] And you don't need a scientific study to know that with two parents rolling up their sleeves, both mothers and fathers will be better rested and more able to relax or to go out for some exercise.

Fathers can play a huge role in promoting equality for women in the home and far beyond. Male leaders in government or business who support policies such as parental leave, good public childcare, and a more flexible approach to paid work can join dads and moms to support these keys to the gender equality revolution.

Why It's Great for Children

Perhaps you're a leader who is in a position to support the greater involvement of fathers and other men in caregiving roles, or perhaps you're a dad yourself. In either case, I hope you're convinced fathers' equal participation is critical to ensure that women have the same opportunities and life possibilities that you have and that it will be good for women's happiness and health. And, from what we saw in the work chapter, I hope you also know it will be great for the economy. But perhaps all that good news won't spur on enough men to support the transformation of fatherhood.

So the next thing men should know is that this is a great thing for children.

There are fatherhood advocates who argue that children *need* a father. You might think I would agree, but let me say this: children actually don't need a father around. I dropped in on the bustling Washington, D.C., office of Gary Barker, international director of Promundo. Gary's PhD was in child and adolescent development and he's also the originator of MenCare, a worldwide campaign that has the goal of men doing one-half of the parenting and care work on the planet.

"Children don't actually need a father around." He pauses for effect. "But then again, you could say that children don't need a mother around either."

What children need, he emphasizes, isn't parenting from people with particular sexual organs. It's endless love and near-endless attention from one or more adults of any sex who are "crazy about that child and their well-being."

For children to feel safe in the world and to emotionally and physically thrive, they require one or more people in their lives who put their needs above everything else, especially when they are very young. They need people who will rush into a blazing fire to save them, work their bones off to feed and clothe them, give positive attention even when they're exhausted, and keep on loving them even when they do really dumb and annoying things. They need cognitive stimulation. They need stability.

This can come from a man and a woman. It can be from two women or two men, a single mother or a single father, or from extended family members.

It makes a lot of sense, since in most cases there is a biological and/or social father in the life of the child, that he plays at least one of those indispensable roles. Part of the reason is that, as every parent knows, children need a staggering amount of attention. It's just damn hard for one person to fill all of a child's physical and emotional needs, especially in their first few years. A single parent who successfully pulls it off is pretty heroic.

But what about the argument that fathers play a unique role in children's lives? For example, it's often pointed out that they tend to play more often and more robustly with kids than do mothers. Numerous studies seem to bear this out.[25]

To get a perspective on this argument, I put the question to University of Cambridge professor Michael Lamb, who has played a critical role over the past four decades in putting research on fatherhood and child development on the map. With his wool sweater and beard, now streaked gray, he looks just the image of the university professor sitting comfortably in his office.

"I once found it appealing to think there were special roles for mothers and fathers," he says. "The problem is that in succeeding decades it became clear this wasn't the case."

But what about the studies that show that fathers engage in more play than mothers?

Michael notes that's true only when you measure by the proportion of their total time with children. But since mothers on average are still spending way more time with children, the average mother plays more with children than dads. And studies in some cultures show that dads are not any more playful than moms at all.[26]

And what about the evidence that playtime with dads is often more stimulating, unpredictable, and arousing?

There may be some truth to this, but it may simply be a symptom of a problem, rather than an argument for fathers' involvement. After all, why might fathers play more robustly? Part of the answer may be the gender divide I spoke about earlier. Because we raise boys and girls differently, we've traditionally learned to act differently, which can include how we play. What's more, some people have speculated that precisely because many men spend much less time with their children, they amp up the volume of interaction when they are with them in order to get the biggest response. They understandably try to compensate for less time with the kids with a bigger injection of energy. And, finally, if the father isn't as often the one to soothe and calm a child down (for nap time, bedtime, or simply quiet time), he is more likely to think that stoking up a kid is cool.

"So why," I ask Michael, "has this idea persisted of fathers' unique role?"

He ponders this for a moment. "It's partly because people want to oversimplify and to find the perfect, simple argument for a father's involvement. And since men often aren't spending as much time with their children as they'd like, they want to believe that the time with them is unique and especially important."

Children do get different things from each parent because they're two different people. But, says Michael, these aren't simply some sort of "gender roles we dragged out of the savannah and remain with us to this day."

"The important features of paternal behavior—warmth, commitment, sensitivity—were the same as the important features of maternal behavior," he writes in one of his articles. "Both relationships shaped children's development, in other words, and there was no evidence [in my research] that the ways in which mothers and fathers affected children's development differed."[27]

However, even if not necessarily unique or indispensable, involved fathers are great for kids, as seen in a number of studies:

- Fathers who did at least 40 percent of family care tasks had children who "had better academic achievement than children whose fathers were less involved."[28]

- Another showed that fathers' greater involvement in routine childcare is associated with children having higher grades in school.[29]
- In economically less advantaged families, where the father was heavily involved, boys showed less aggressive behavior. In these families, both boys and girls showed less delinquency when they became young adults. A study of disadvantaged African American families showed that in families with highly engaged dads, children had "significantly higher IQ scores at three years of age." These beneficial effects were not only among the less well-off. In economically advantaged families with highly engaged fathers, children showed "less behavioral problems during the early school years."[30]
- Other studies of the impact on children of greater father participation show enhanced cognitive development during infancy and better average social functioning during childhood and as adults.[31]

British researcher and fatherhood advocate Adrienne Burgess of the Fatherhood Institute is almost brusque in her dismissal of anyone who doesn't think that a loving, active father can't make a difference for children. She hands me a study she's done that pulls together a huge amount of data. In it, she says, "The positive outcomes include better peer relationships; fewer behaviour problems; lower criminality and substance abuse; higher educational/occupational mobility relative to parents' employment; capacity for empathy; non-traditional attitudes to earning and childcare; more satisfying adult sexual partnerships; and higher self-esteem and life-satisfaction."[32]

Of course, Adrienne is quick to add that it isn't just about quantity, but the quality of fathers' care. A domineering or verbally or physically abusive father (or mother for that matter) will have a negative impact on a child's emotional and intellectual development. But good-quality care pays off, in both the short and long term. For example, one study showed that "children of warm affectionate fathers [were] more likely to be coping well at age forty-one, and to be mentally healthy and psychologically mature." And how close children, especially girls, were to their father at sixteen was a strong predictor of their future marital satisfaction and psychological well-being.[33]

Given the important role that dads can play in the lives of their children, it's particularly sad to see that only 42 percent of separated and divorced women in the United States received the full child support they were due. And almost one-third, 29.5 percent, received not a penny of the child support they were due.[34]

Luckily, the majority of fathers take their responsibilities seriously. And as we've seen, more and more dads are putting their responsibilities in the home on par with or even above their responsibilities at work.

Dramatic changes in men's roles as caregivers will cause sweeping changes in the coming generations. Girls with more equitable fathers or other adult male caregivers show lower rates of experiencing unwanted sex. Boys benefit from having a positive role model in their caring father. They are more likely to support gender equality. Girls benefit from seeing both parents do the work at home—one study found that daughters with parents "who share domestic chores equally are more likely to aspire to less traditional, and potentially higher paying, jobs."[35]

A healthy father-child relationship and sense of security helps children develop to their full potential. As my coauthors and I wrote in *State of the World's Fathers*, involved fatherhood also contributes "to boys' acceptance of gender equality and to girls' sense of autonomy and empowerment." It can contribute to ensuring that all children are protected from violence, abuse, exploitation, and neglect and enjoy their right to protection, survival, education, development, and participation. If they "see their fathers in a respectful, non-violent, equitable relationship with their mothers and other women," including participation in domestic duties and decision making, both boys and girls "internalize the idea that men and women are equal [and] pass this on to their own children."[36]

That deep bond can be there forever.

From the Start to Infinity: Why It's Important for Men

I'm a long way from the North American stores where dads and moms line up to drop hundreds of dollars on a stroller. I'm visiting a maternity clinic in the sprawling township of

Khayelitsha outside of Cape Town, South Africa. Physically, it's a grim community. Most of its four hundred thousand inhabitants live in densely packed shacks with no running water, the only nod to modernity being the jumble of electrical wires that show one of the big improvements since the end of apartheid.

Solonzi is in his midtwenties and his smile has a nice way of sharpening his already prominent cheekbones. He's wearing narrow-legged olive-green cargo pants and a dark blue fleece. His girlfriend is due within weeks. He's anxiously awaiting news that he'll land a job as a parking lot attendant.

"My father?" he says in response to my question. "I only met him. Just once. All I know about him is his name."

Solonzi says, "I always thought, if I have a child, I don't want someone else to experience what I did. I want my baby to get every attention from me. I'm willing to learn everything, changing nappies, everything. I don't mind cleaning. I already do most of the cooking"—and here he smiles shyly—"because she likes my cooking."

What type of father will he be?

His look is serious, but then he smiles, once again highlighting those cheekbones. "For my baby, I will do everything," he says. "From the start to infinity."[37]

We know that equal participation by men in caring for kids and doing our share of housework is great for women and children. But let's say you still aren't completely convinced, or perhaps other priorities and demands keep getting in the way.

So let's marshal the final bit of evidence to encourage all men to support men taking on half of the care work.

Slogging away as a father is really great for men too. And not just for those men who actually happen to be fathers at the time. This might seem counterintuitive. Doesn't it impinge on your career and get in the way of the work you love or the necessity of putting in extra hours at work? Won't it cut into your chances to relax, hit the gym, or hang out with friends? Why not just spend some good quality time with the kids?

Remember what I wrote earlier of the paradox of men's power? The very ways we have set up a society of men's power certainly brings rewards to men, but it comes with a terrible price. Remember the men who no longer have their careers, who said they did it all for their family but now that they're retired, feel they don't even know their own kids? You know, *when it comes to being a good dad, I could have been a contender.*

The gender equality advantage to men of playing a much greater role in the home goes way beyond those negatives.

When I interview fathers, or just ask them in conversation about their experiences as a dad, there is often a mad jumble of words, as if they're trying to piece together an experience that was, until then, beyond comprehension or expectation.

Life-changing is a phrase I hear over and over.

I never thought I could ever love someone so much.

Joe, who lives in the mountains of Virginia, says, "It's just so extraordinary to watch him. It's the same stuff that kids everywhere do, I know that on an intellectual level. But every time he learns a new word it's the most fascinating thing on earth."

A Russian father I interviewed in St. Petersburg talked about the responsibility. "Fatherhood made me more conscious of the things I do. I needed always to be conscious of the consequences of my actions."

Fathers, like mothers, are quick to admit it's exhausting and boring and financially stressful. There can be new stresses in relationships. Joe says, "For the first time, [my wife and I] we're short with each other, never before. We were sleep-deprived, frustrated with things happening."

Eric, an IT specialist working with a San Francisco start-up, says that his hour-long metro commute became a time to catch up on sleep rather than work.

Interviews with fathers by my White Ribbon colleagues detail how they've lost spontaneity and a sense of control over their lives. As children got older, there was a bucketful of new stresses and concerns.[38]

Meanwhile, many dads have to fight through incomprehension or skepticism from family members or colleagues about their role as a dad. One father, Stephen, told me, "When I told my parents I'd be looking after our son while my wife worked, they asked me what I was going to do with him all day. Really?"

No, it's not always fun. But like millions and millions of fathers, grandfathers, uncles, friends, and other men who play a caregiving role in the lives of children they love, the fathers I've spoken to said it was the best thing in their lives.

In many studies, dads speak of "a new level of authenticity" and "a profound shift from 'me' to 'we.'"[39] One re-searcher writes: "The more men engaged with their children, the more satisfied they were with their lives, the more social-izing they did, the more involved they were in their commu-nities, the more connected they were with their families, and the less involved they were with their work."[40]

Fathers report "a heightened sense of maturity, new em-pathic abilities, and greater self-confidence . . . a sense of be-coming a more complete and secure person."[41]

That increased empathy can be draining. Stephen says to me, "I can't listen or hear about bad news. I see it all now through the lens of my son and all children now. I hear news from Syria and it just kills me. This makes it tough for a political junkie like me. But I just can't watch anything with gore—where anyone is in peril."

In other words, as the author of one study concludes, "Emotional reciprocity and shared play in the context of a loving relationship with a child plays a key role in men's own development."[42]

This development is truly transformational. As former US vice president Joe Biden once said, "Looking back on it, the truth be told, the real reason I went home every night was that I needed my children more than they needed me."

These changes can have a profound cascading effect on men. Fathers quit smoking at a higher rate than other men.[43] Fathers take their health more seriously and reduce risk-taking behavior.[44]

In spite of the many new pressures, fatherhood can have a positive impact on mental health. A West Coast dad named Cameron tells me he got very depressed after being fired from his media job. Suddenly he was at home all day. It was only later that he realized that "my time with my toddler was what got me through." And Cameron adds, "By the way, I hate the term *involved father*. We'd never dream of saying *involved mother*."

Fatherhood can open up a whole new world for men. My colleague Mats Berggren from the Swedish organization Men for Gender Equality tells me about a fathers' group he led in Ethiopia. One man said, "You talk really strange. We don't understand this gender equality talk." But then the man pointed to his heart: "But we realize we long for it inside." Another man started crying. "Why didn't we think about this before?"

Men's caregiving: Good for women. Good for children. Good for men.

More than any single thing, the transformation of fatherhood shows the advantage to men that flows from gender equality.

Why Are Fathers' Roles Changing?

We usually focus on how changes in women's lives—in particular, the explosion of women in the workforce—have been the impetus for changes in our families. Over the past fifty years, women's aspirations have clearly changed—more and more women began to focus on higher education and careers. And the advent of safe and effective birth control and, at least in some places, access to safe therapeutic abortion means that women can make decisions about if and when to have children.

Indeed, the feminist revolution is the main impetus for changes in the role of fathers. With more women in the workforce or pursuing higher education, new demands are plunked on men in the home.

But we often forget about men within the change equation.

Over the past few decades, as mechanization led to a de-skilling of jobs that men disproportionately enjoyed, as rates of unionization plummeted and real wages went down, and as government-provided social services decreased and family expenses increased under the onslaught of economic policies pursued by conservative and liberal governments alike, fewer and fewer men had the ability to earn a wage that could support a whole family. The days of the so-called family wage were over. And so, women not only wanted to but also needed to be working outside the home.

Meanwhile, many men lost their jobs or were forced into part-time work as a result of the 2008 recession or the ongoing impact of globalization. Many found themselves at home while their wives were out working.

But there has also been a positive impetus for changes in fathers' roles. One of the things accomplished by the massive cultural upheavals of the 1960s and 1970s was a questioning among men about their devotion to a job and career over family and relationships. Even though it has been different from the generational revolt among women, there certainly has been a generational revolt among men. Meanwhile, those same men are getting challenged and pushed by increasingly well-educated and independently minded women. Among the challenges? To share work in the home, including the work of looking after children.

These days, more and more men take these changes for granted. Women were elbowing their way *into* men's traditional territory just as other social, economic, and political forces were pushing men *out of* our traditional breadwinner role. Men were questioning our traditional role in the nuclear family at the very same time women were challenging us to play a different one. And men started figuring out that a good relationship with a spouse and close ties with children were far more important than our jobs. On that score, men were becoming more like women. The Pew Research Center asked US women and men how marriage, children, and careers fit into their priorities. The results from women might have been expected. When asked what was important or very important to them, 94 percent of women said being a good parent, 84 percent said a successful marriage, while only 51 percent said success in a high-paying career or profession. The results from men were more surprising: 91 percent said being a good parent, 83 percent a successful marriage, and only 49 percent said success in a high-paying career or profession.[45]

It's a change we're seeing around the world. Remember my mention of Kipsigis fathers in Kenya who never hold a baby? The same is true in parts of nearby Rwanda where women have resisted encouraging their husbands to hold babies or even be around them until they're old enough to walk. When my colleagues from Promundo and the Rwanda Men's Resource Centre went into different communities, many expectant fathers or dads with newborns said they'd never held a baby, which was just as expected. But what they said next took my colleagues by surprise. The men said, "We want to learn. We want to learn how to hold and feed our babies."

However, it's not enough to say that change is happening. Change can also *un*happen, or move way too slowly. How can we speed up the process of positive change? And how can we ensure that any change is beneficial to the greatest number of women, men, and children?

Be the Change

In Stockholm I'm visiting a group for new and expectant dads. They're meeting each week to explore the challenges they will face (or are facing) as fathers. They're picking up parenting skills. They're discussing how this is affecting their relationships. All these fathers, like almost all fathers in the Scandinavian countries, will take weeks or even months off work, receiving about 80 percent of their pay, to look after their new child.

The four dads with me that night are in their twenties or early thirties and part of the Swedish generation for whom paternity leave is as normal as smoked salmon.

One of them is Magnus, a big man with close-cropped hair and imposing strength. He paves roads for a living, but right now, with his baby seven months old, he's working four days a week. I ask how his employer feels about this, and he replies, "They like it when we're happy."

But what truly astounds me is his story about visiting his hometown. "It's in a conservative part of Sweden," he says. "Our Bible Belt." I immediately imagine the Tea Party except they speak Swedish. "I was home recently," he continues, "and met up with my old friends. I told them that when my girl is nine months old, my wife's going back to work and I'm gonna take seven months off. They thought this was really weird."

Seven months off? Definitely would seem weird, I thought. After all, this is the conservative part of his country.

But Magnus continues. "When I said I was gonna take seven months off, they said, 'Why don't you just take off the normal two or three months?'"

He cannot understand why I'm laughing.

"What's so funny?" he asks.

I explain that in the rest of the world, men taking two months' leave (let alone seven months) is either a pipe dream or wouldn't even occur to them. Many would be lucky to have seven days.

No one in the group can understand why I'm so astounded. Highly involved fatherhood is all that they've ever known.

For these men, being counted in is part of who they are and what they have always known.

Their story gives us some important clues about promoting change. On the most basic level, just as those Swedish men have been encouraged, we need to encourage fathers everywhere to make a personal commitment to take on half the care work. This means different things to different men, and different things as we go through our lives. However, it always means taking the personal risk to do some introspection. To ask ourselves uncomfortable questions about our priorities, our relationship, and our own experiences when we were children. To get feedback from our spouse and, as they grow up, from our children or the children we're taking some responsibility for. And to develop sustainable plans.

A commitment to personal change isn't a once-in-a-lifetime-and-then-you're-done proposition. I'm not saying you've got to slog through your life constantly trying to improve yourself. But given that we're all products of a male-dominated world where men's roles as parents have been secondary, change is something that we need to keep our eye on, as one story shows.

I'm sitting at my kitchen table with Ziauddin Yousafzai, the father of Nobel Peace Prize winner Malala Yousafzai. Ziauddin is a longtime supporter of women's rights and, especially, girls' education. He assumed he was putting his own life in danger by admitting girls to his school against the threats of the Taliban—and never imagined they would attack his daughter instead. Malala herself credits him for inspiring her. So you'd think that Ziauddin would have things pretty worked out when it comes to new roles for fathers and getting rid of tired old sexist assumptions.

But he tells me this story about how our own background, assumptions, and gender biases keep raising their head from time to time. This was a few years ago when Malala was around fifteen and still in high school in England. "I was in the car with my family," he told me. "I said to my son, who is younger than Malala, 'I'm going to be away, so you're supposed to be head of the family.' Malala looked at me the way only a teenager can look at you. And I said, 'I didn't mean that, I didn't mean that.'" His eyes sparkle as he laughs at himself. He then grows serious. "For change, we must unlearn things. The change has to start with us."

However, as the story of the Swedish fathers shows, this isn't about throwing men in the deep end and expecting them to know how to swim. Both as families and as a society, we need to help dads develop the skills, tools, *and* mindset to be active dads. After all, most men in the world grew up seeing their father playing a secondary role as a parent—many men simply don't have a model of what it means to be an equal partner in looking after children. And as children, we certainly didn't integrate caregiving into our games. I mean, I was out in the woods with my friends playing war games and learning to shoot imaginary guns and die dramatic deaths— there was one huge sand hill where my cousin lived that was particularly effective—while our sisters were practicing nurturing skills on their dolls or looking after younger siblings.

I've talked to many fathers about making a commitment to do the hard work of change—and there's so much we need to learn. I question the focus on "quality time," a buzz phrase that often leaves women doing most of the work while dads get to do the fun stuff. (And besides, it's often in the midst of the daily chores that, out of the blue, you'll have those amazing talks with your kids.) I've visited fathers' groups that teach men about the importance of doing audits to see which parent does which housekeeping jobs, who organizes housework, and how much time it takes—followed by developing a plan to share jobs equally. I see dads pushing for the social supports they need to play an equal role in the home: better government and company parental leave, pushing employers to enact family-friendly policies, and supporting political candidates who will work for government-backed parental leave and accessible, low-cost, high-quality, not-for-profit childcare.

We need opportunities to help men learn about the realities and challenges of fatherhood. I meet up with Danish psychiatrist Svend Aage Madsen at the maternity ward of Copenhagen University Hospital (where patient rooms include a small bed for dads or other partners to sleep at night). As well as his own clinical practice, Svend has done extensive interviews with mothers and fathers. "Before birth," he says, "when men talked about their coming child, 85 percent talked about much bigger children. Running around, playing football, bicycling. Meanwhile, 90 percent of moms talked about infants. But here's the thing. In interviews after the birth, 85 percent of men talked about infants. They realized their earlier ideas were way off."

Fathers groups and positive parenting programs provide not only an avenue for learning about the realities of parenting and a place to talk about new challenges, but they also sometimes give men an experience with other men that they've never had before. Mark Osborn has led fatherhood groups in England, often for men who've had fewer social and economic opportunities. He tells me of one of the many dads he worked with in groups. "There's one father, a big bloke, skinhead and tattoos. The other staff were really anxious about him. He was quiet through the whole first session. Until at the very end when we asked the dads what they want from this group. And he said, 'Love.' He was looking for some safety that he'd never had."

I've heard the same thing from middle-class or wealthy fathers.

Meanwhile, one of the concerns I've heard from some fathers (and mothers) is that some women are too quick to jump to the rescue. Baby cries in Dad's arms; Mom takes the baby. Dad is a bit clumsy at first feeding the baby or choosing the right clothes for the toddler, and Mom jumps in. A supportive family environment is one that supports men learning the caregiving skills they may never have learned before.

In a way, however, if we wait until men become fathers to give them the tools and help them develop a caregiving mindset, we've waited too long. Why not start young and understand the diverse range of activities and programs that will contribute to this goal?

Some examples are obvious, such as parenting and babysitting programs in high schools. We can start with little children, though, helping them develop nurturing skills and increase their social and emotional competence. For example, the wonderful Roots of Empathy program is structured around bringing a baby into an elementary classroom.[46] We can encourage caregiving opportunities for students through mentoring of younger students, peer-to-peer support, and carefully focused volunteer work in the community. Educators must ensure that schoolbooks and images on classroom walls equally show women and men in caregiving roles.

We need to include sexuality education in order to bring about lasting change. Healthy families start with healthy relationships among the parents and that, in turn, requires shared sexual decision making and responsibility. But in the United States, one study suggests that an astounding 30 percent of teenage boys had sexual intercourse *before* receiving any sexuality education.[47] It shouldn't surprise us that unplanned pregnancies and sexually transmitted infections decrease among those who've had sexuality education.[48] And yet, in the United States, twenty-six states don't require public schools to teach sexual education.[49] In many places where there is something that passes as sex ed, it focuses on body parts and diseases and doesn't invite young people into a comprehensive education that includes sexual behavior, communication, contraception, body image, pleasure, sexual orientation, gender identity, and much more. Instead it gets loaded up with moralizing abstinence education that doesn't teach responsible decision making and leaves young people ill-prepared for the realities of their lives.[50]

And in the home, parents can make sure that children's household responsibilities aren't gender-coded and that any jobs get shared out. This is not only to model gender equality and respect for all jobs, but to ensure that both our girls and boys develop all they need for self-sufficiency and also to live gender-equitable lives in the future. Children can also be brought into age-appropriate discussions around household tasks and even budgeting so they can experience shared decision making firsthand.

Not Only by Your Own Bootstraps

We wrongly assume that personal change—in this case, men playing an equal role in caregiving—is simply about personal volition. That fits well with our lasting images of the self-made man who tirelessly and wordlessly gets on with the job.

But it just ain't so.

Magnus, that Swedish father who paved roads, wasn't taking seven months off his paid work to look after his child simply because he wanted to. Nor did the idea pop into his head out of the blue. He did it because government policies enabled him to. And because government policies enabled him, he, like millions of other men in so many countries, has shifted his priorities. That is, a set of new laws shifted the social norm in his country. What was unusual thirty years ago had become the norm today.

All men must voice our strong support for government policies that will transform men's (and women's) abilities to be good parents and create a better start for our children.

Most countries have government-mandated and funded parental leave programs. Only three (plus a few tiny Pacific islands) do not: the United States (per capita GDP $55,840), Papua New Guinea (per capital GDP $2,270) and Lesotho (per capita GDP $1,030). These are the only countries that don't give parents the right to paid parental leave and support it with a state-funded program.

The problem, says one Silicon Valley father (whose company offers decent paid parental leave that he has taken advantage of), is that without state policies and programs, "Leave is more a rich persons' thing these days."

If you're a parent working at a minimum-wage job, you simply don't have any cushion to take off much, if any, time. I spoke to one man working on a gardening crew: he took two days off when his first child was born and that was only by phoning in sick.

Parental leave programs vary dramatically from country to country. The gold standard is the Nordic countries. For example, Swedish parents are now entitled to 480 paid days shared between them. Yes, sixty-eight and a half weeks. Meanwhile, the United Kingdom now has up to fifty weeks of parental leave, thirty-seven weeks of them paid—and this includes same-sex, adoptive, and nonbiological cohabiting parents.

In the absence of any federal commitment, some US states and cities are taking action:

- California, the United States' largest economy, has Paid Family Leave, which requires employers to provide up to six weeks of wage replacement for caregiving, either to a new child or an ill family member.
- New York, the third-largest economy, guarantees its citizens eight weeks of paid, job-protected leave for caregiving needs, increasing to twelve weeks of paid leave in 2021.

- New Jersey, Rhode Island, and Washington, D.C., also have paid leave.
- Boston, Minneapolis, Cincinnati, New York City, and Portland, Oregon, are among those that have paid family leave for municipal employees.

Some companies resist paid leave on the assumption that this will hit their bottom lines. But when they were surveyed after the implementation of California's Paid Family Leave program, 87 percent of companies "reported that there were no cost increases, and some even reported a reduction in costs due to lower employee turnover."[51]

All this is fine. But even the most generous policies don't mean that dads are going to step up to the plate. Too many tired old ideas stand in the way. Parents and everyone around them assume that the mother is the natural parent. Dads worry about employer fallout if they take time off. Men fret they'll be socially isolated and will be the only guy in the children's play group or pediatrician's office. Add on economic disincentives: since men on average make more than women, for many couples debating who will take off time, it's a no-brainer.

What can we do, then, to help ensure that fathers will be part of this historic change?

I'm in Tromso, Norway, north of the Arctic Circle. It's a small but prosperous city and, due to the Gulf Stream, pleasantly warm. And since it's the end of June, the sun shines and people are up around the clock. It's late in the evening and I'm on a fishing boat with a group of friends and colleagues.

We pull cod out of the icy waters and the boat captain steams them and we dig in. I've never had such fresh fish.

We're all in town to attend a conference and so it's no surprise that my discussion with my colleagues Jorgen Lorentzen and Øystein Holter turns to work. I ask them about what accounts for the big uptick in fathers taking parental leave.

The answer came without a moment's hesitation. Although Norway had included fathers in paid parental leave since the late 1970s, men's participation had been low. Then in 1993 some policy makers came up with the clever idea of a father's quota. Four weeks of parental leave were assigned directly to fathers (later rising to six weeks.) An equal chunk was reserved for mothers and the rest would be shared as a couple saw fit. Fathers taking paid leave jumped from only 4 percent to 89 percent by 2012.[52] Daddy days were born.

Since then, the policy has slowly spread. In Iceland, for example, moms are entitled to three months off, a father (or a second female parent) to three months off, and three additional months can be shared. The average father now takes 103 days of paid parental leave.

These policies have put down strong roots in North America, specifically in the Canadian province of Quebec. Until 2006, parents were covered under a Canada-wide plan that was already quite decent. But that year, the province introduced its own plan. They hiked benefits by 50 percent. They reasoned that many parents no longer had old-style jobs, so they extended benefits to temporary, seasonal, and self-employed workers. Under the Canadian plan there was an unpaid "waiting period" before benefits started; they dumped that. They made things more flexible and let parents choose whether to go with forty weeks of leave (at 75 percent of salary) or fifty-five weeks (at 70 percent of salary.) And perhaps most important of all, nontransferable daddy days were introduced, which reserved five weeks exclusively for the father.

Here's what happened. Before the new law, Quebec already boasted the highest rate of Canadian dads taking leave: 22 percent of fathers compared to 9 percent in the rest of Canada. (That's not including a week or two after the birth of a child.) With the new policy, numbers soared. In the first year they jumped to 56 percent of dads. By 2011, it was 84 percent of dads. The rest of Canada? Stuck at 11 percent.[53]

It's a great example of how social policies can have a big, positive effect. And it's why I'm pleased that the Canadian government is introducing nontransferable father's days across the country.

All this is why men—not only those in government, but those of us who elect governments—need to be pressing hard for government action:

- *Introduce parental leave*: In the United States, the number one policy that will support parents, promote gender equality at home and indirectly at work, and boost the role of fathers is a national parental leave program. Working people in the United States deserve nothing less than what their counterparts across Europe and around the world also have.

- *Improve parental leave:* Increase the period of leave and percentage of wages that are covered. Make it more flexible so, for example, a couple can both work half time. Include self-employed, part-time, and marginally employed workers. Make it inclusive of all parents, of all sexual orientations and gender identities.

- *Nontransferable daddy days:* Introduce a use-it-or-lose-it portion of total parental leave that can be used only by a father (or another second parent).

- *Childcare policies and programs:* Our children and our parents deserve government programs that support high-quality, low-cost, accessible, not-for-profit, licensed day care.

- *Data collection:* Knowledge is critical to map out the current household work of women and men and to evaluate the impact of programs on bringing about greater equality. Governments can contribute by collecting better time-use data for men and women.[54]

Unfortunately, in the United States, government support for parental leave is still weak. Despite all the pious political statements about strong families, moms and dads are always left in the lurch, whether from the lack of affordable, accessible, quality childcare or well-paid and lengthy parental leave . . . well, any parental leave, for that matter. And so, until parents win those things across the country, companies will have a particular role in picking up the slack. Companies, unions, and professional associations must urgently put a focus on having employers provide paid parental leave and sick time to look after children and sick family members. Similarly, where possible, they need to introduce parent-friendly policies, like flexible hours and working from home, taking care to avoid scheduling meetings during school drop-off and pick-up times, providing workplace childcare, and supporting breastfeeding moms.

Transforming Fatherhood: A Pathway to Gender Equality and Better Lives for Men

The interesting thing is how much these types of changes, and in particular nontransferable parental leave for fathers, can promote gender equality. A Swedish study showed that every month of father's leave increased a mother's income by 6.7 percent, as measured four years later.[55] But the promotion of household gender equality goes beyond those who took leave. Some researchers compared men and women who became parents during the two years leading up to the father's quota and those who became parents in the first two years after the quota. They visited these families twenty years later. Attitudes to gender equality were pretty much the same in the two groups, which isn't surprising since they're basically the same age cohort. But it seems that the daddy days converted sentiment to action: among the post–daddy day parents— now with grown children—the odds that couples still divided household work equally was 50 percent higher. And the amazing thing was that this was true even among parents where the dad did *not* take any leave. In other words, the policy contributed to broader, pro-equality social change.[56]

Nothing is going to be more transformative in promoting gender equality and women's rights than men doing half of the care work. British actor Charlie Condou is one man who wants to be counted in. He talks openly about his own painful childhood, one that included the imprisonment of his father when he was only a baby. For as long as he can remember, he wanted to be a father. "I had a fantasy as a kid about reaching into a car and picking my son out and carrying him very quietly upstairs and feeling his breath on my neck and putting him to bed."

Charlie is now a father of two children. "Kids are like giant snowballs rolling down a mountain," he says. "It gets bigger and bigger and goes faster and faster. If you try to stand in front of it and stop it, it will knock you over and keep going the way it's going anyway—picking up everything, learning. Your job next to children is to run alongside saying, are you okay, are you okay, and make sure it doesn't bang into trees and rocks."

For individual men, being counted in to join the gender equality revolution may or may not include fatherhood.

But when it comes to embracing and supporting the world of caregiving in all its forms, it certainly requires rethinking our priorities as men. And it requires rethinking the priorities of our world.

Cary Area Public Library
1606 Three Oaks Road
Cary, IL 60013

6

ARMISTICE DAY

Men Can End the War Against Women

My father, a gentle, strong, and loving man, and my mother, a gentle, strong, and loving woman, both carried a great delight for life, a great delight for their children, and a great delight for each other. Except for their annual argument for a few minutes on the evening they wrestled with their income tax preparations, I never heard either of them express annoyance with each other, let alone raise their voices, let alone raise a fist.

Back in the 1950s and 1960s when I was living in Cleveland, Ohio; Durham, North Carolina; and then Kingston, Ontario, violence against women wasn't something you read about in the paper—except when I lived in the South and an African American man would be charged, often without evidence, with violence against a white woman.

Violence against women was kept invisible. Wife battering was seen as a private matter between husband and wife.

Terms like *date rape* and *sexual harassment* didn't exist, although both acts certainly did. It was still legal for a man to rape his wife[1]—in fact, it wasn't until 1993 that Oklahoma and North Carolina became the last states to finally criminalize marital rape; in Canada it was only ten years earlier.

Thus, like so many men, whether because I grew up in a loving household and assumed all homes were like mine or because violence against women was barely touched in the media, courts, or halls of government, I had no clue about the magnitude of the problem. But then things began to change. Courageous women in different countries started to push governments in the 1970s for more effective laws and insisted that police and prosecutors implement those laws. They set up crisis centers and shelters to help women escape violent relationships.

And they pushed to raise awareness about the staggering amount of violence against women.

Imagine this: You are visiting a city in Peru and find yourself sitting at an outdoor café. Cars bustle along, pedestrians flock the streets, a couple of dogs trot by. You start counting the women going by in cars, in buses, or walking along the sidewalk. Let's imagine you can somehow count only the women who have been in an intimate partnership with a man.

You count one hundred such women.

How many, you ask, have experienced physical or sexual violence from a partner?

The answer is fifty-one of them, every other woman who walks by on this day in a small city in Peru. There's certainly no disease that could affect a number like that (especially when you include both the young and the old). Not cancer or heart disease, not tuberculosis or AIDS. In fact, not all of those things combined. Half of the adult women in Peru do *not* have those diseases, but half of them have experienced violence at the hands of a husband or live-in boyfriend.

Peru isn't the worst country in the world for violence against women, although it is worse than average.

An in-depth study done in ten countries by the World Health Organization between 2004 and 2005 paints a grim picture—and little has changed since.

If you were to do the same counting exercise in a provincial town in Brazil, the number would be thirty-seven, or about one in three. In a city in Serbia or Montenegro, it's one in four. Even in Japan, with one of the lowest rates in the world—far lower than the United States, Canada, or England, for example—it's still an astonishing one in every six women who passes by.

In the United States, the 2017 National Intimate Partner and Sexual Violence Survey from the Centers for Disease Control shows the enormity of the problem. One in four women has experienced *severe* physical violence by an intimate partner. One in ten women has been raped by an intimate partner.[2]

Government statistics point to 4.8 million physical assaults and rapes against women in intimate relations each year in the United States.[3] In the time it takes you to read this short paragraph, two women were beaten or raped.

A massive and rigorous European study released in 2014

reported unthinkable figures: In the year before the survey was released, an estimated 13 million women in the European Union had experienced physical violence; 3.7 million experienced sexual violence. That's 8 percent of European women in one year alone. Almost one in three women experienced physical violence since the age of fifteen, and 11 percent experienced some form of sexual violence.[4]

Let's not ignore psychological violence in relationships. These include forbidding a woman to leave the house, making her watch porn against her wishes, scaring or intimidating her on purpose, threatening her with violence, threatening to hurt someone she loves or destroy something she cares about, and constantly humiliating and belittling her in private or in public. That same European study discovered that 32 percent of women experienced one or more of these.[5]

Stalking? Nine million European women, or 5 percent of the women surveyed, were stalked in the year before their survey interview. In all, 18 percent of women have been stalked. One in five of these victims had to change their phone numbers and email addresses.[6]

Murder? Gloria Steinem points out that in the decade following 9/11, more US women were murdered by a current or former intimate partner than the number of people killed in the attack on the Twin Towers *plus* the number of Americans killed in Afghanistan and Iraq. In fact, it's almost twice as many—15,462 versus 9,838, which is not to minimize how horrible the latter was, but to show the level of the former.[7] Within the United Kingdom, in England and Wales alone, a woman was murdered by a man every two and a half days between 2009 and the end of 2015.[8]

These are numbers, and numbers have a tendency to blur. So imagine we are talking about the women you know.

While violence against women might seem like a problem half a world away, it's also a problem half a block away. Or next door. Or in your own home. "I didn't think much about this thing," said one middle-aged man to me. "Until my daughter came home with her cheek swollen and tears in her eyes." He stopped talking, his face suddenly washed over with defeat. Finally, he said that her boyfriend had punched her because he thought she was flirting with another guy at a party.

The violence is this:

I am smack in the middle of Minnesota, in the middle of the United States, in a town that's big enough to have its share of fast-food restaurants and also a woman's shelter. It's a cold winter morning and I have to use a credit card to scrape frost off the windshield of my rented car before I can drive to that shelter. The women who had organized my community talk the night before are justifiably proud to show me their new building and tell me about opportunities they are giving women from their town and the surrounding farms. We drink coffee and eat sticky sweet pastries. It could be a small office just about anywhere in North America, except, that is, when they start conferring among themselves about the women who are coming in. Women who, with their husbands, run farms. Women who work in those fast-food restaurants. Women who are housewives with well-off husbands. Women who work in the local meat-processing plant, who teach, who manage bank branches. Some of these women had stuck around for twenty years of beatings until their children grew up; others were able to get out after a few months; for none of them has it been easy.

Meanwhile, across the border in Canada, according to government surveys, 25 percent of women are victims of physical violence from a partner at least once in their lives.

I am driving through Rome in a beat-up Fiat with two women who help women escape abusive relationships. A young Chinese woman is with them, but I haven't been introduced and she hasn't said a word. I glance back at her again and can't decide if she is sixteen or thirty. She smokes yet another cigarette and barely answers when I say hello to her in Chinese. Later, the other women explain: she is among the hundreds of thousands trafficked each year into prostitution. Many are lured away with promises of good jobs and then find themselves locked up and repeatedly raped into submission. They may be thousands of miles from home, without a passport or an ability to speak the local language, without knowledge of their rights, fearful of what will happen to them or their families if they try to escape. This young woman did escape, although judging by the hard look in her eyes, she has a long way to go before she will be free.

I'm in London at the home of a friend and colleague, Maggie Baxter, who at the time headed a women's rights organization. We're talking with a woman from Sudan who has dedicated her life to ending female genital mutilation. Each month 170,000 girls in east and central Africa undergo these horrific procedures. According to the latest figures from UNICEF and the UNFPA, 200 million women and girls alive today have been genitally cut; 44 million of those are fourteen or younger.[9]

I am in India where I'm speaking to colleagues from Save the Children. They work on many issues concerning violence against women and children, but one critical problem is the impact on children who witness violence against their mothers. Research tells us that when young children witness violence against a loved one, it tends to have the same emotional impact as if it happened directly against them. It turns out that violence against women in the home quickly becomes a form of deep emotional violence against children. Each year, tens of millions of children experience violence against their own mother and some against their father.

For too long women carried the burden of this violence. They carried it in bruises and broken bones; they carried it in their minds and their souls. Some carried it to their graves.

A War Against Women?

How can we find the language to capture the plight of hundreds of millions of women around the world? When we speak about violence against women, we often turn to metaphors.[10] It's a war. It's like a pandemic disease (meaning occurring over a wide area and affecting a significant part of the population); there's an "epidemic of the violence"; women are "afflicted" by the violence, as if it were something nasty they caught when their husband sneezed.

When we use metaphors like *the war on women*, some people object that no one has ever declared a war on women. True, although women have long been victims within wars, often targeted for rape, sometimes on an organized, mass scale, as we saw in recent years on at least three continents—in the Democratic Republic of the Congo throughout the first years of this century, in Bosnia at the end of the last, in Bangladesh during its war of independence in 1971. But these were not wars fought with the view of subjugating women; women were used as sexual fodder, as a statement of men's power, as a way of dehumanizing the "enemy," of further brutalizing the soldiers themselves, as a way of terrorizing and humiliating both those women and the population as a whole.

Similarly, the college-age man who pressures and pressures, who keeps pouring alcohol until, finally, his date is in no position to give informed consent to having sex, and who then goes ahead and has sex with his inebriated partner isn't looking for war, he is looking for sexual satisfaction—well, to be precise, *his* sexual satisfaction. Even the wife who is terrified of the consequences if she says no to her husband (even though at that moment she doesn't want to have sex) isn't a victim of war, although she may feel like a prisoner in her own bed.

The woman who is hit by her husband may also be economically dependent on him (and, indeed, this can be one reason why it is difficult for a woman to pack up and escape with her children). The woman who is hit may also, at other times, experience love and connection with her husband.

Certainly the issue is multifaceted and complex. And

true, most men don't rape or murder; the majority of men would never dream of hitting their wife or girlfriend.

Yet the image of a war against women is indelible. This war has directly touched the bodies of a quarter to a third of adult women on the planet. And because of its magnitude, many others have to go through their days knowing this could happen to them. Such knowledge affects the daily behavior and peace of mind of women everywhere, from the university student who has to think twice about going home alone from the library or who gives a friend her detailed plans for the evening before going out on a first date, to the village woman who can't fetch water from a distant well until she has others to accompany her.

And because many men (and an equal number of women) have experienced violence in their homes when they were children, either directly to their bodies or because it's happening against their mother, violence has had a direct impact on many men as well.

Who Are These Men Who Commit Violence?

It's a question I have posed so many times to the experts, women who work in shelters for battered women and in rape crisis centers and who answer help lines and speak to women in their deepest moments of distress. It is a question I've asked police officers and psychologists. It's a question I ask researchers. Whether I ask that question in Iowa or Ireland or Indonesia, I get the same sort of answer: the men who commit violence are farmers and doctors, office workers and company presidents, soldiers and athletes, stockbrokers and factory workers, police officers and ministers, truck drivers and students. It is true that in some cultures, in some countries, the problem is worse than in others because abuse may be more widely tolerated, or laws are more lax, or the women's movement hasn't yet had the impact it has elsewhere. But there is no country, no social class, no occupation that is immune— although we will see there are a few small cultures in which violence against women is very rare.

Men who commit acts of violence against women, who bully their girlfriend or hit their wife, are men who disproportionately had a father or stepfather who was abusive against his mother. Now let's be clear: there are many men who lived with abuse in their childhood homes who will never use violence themselves. In fact, many heroic boys and young men eventually stood up to an abusive father—there is true resiliency in their lives. But if you want to find one factor that predicts whether a boy will grow up to be a man who uses violence, it's experiencing violence in his childhood home. This has been confirmed in studies all over the world, including my colleagues' International Men and Gender Equality Survey.[11] And government research in Canada shows that boys who experience violence by their fathers are three times more likely to commit violence against their spouses compared to those who do not.

A child-support worker told me about one case. A man was arrested for strangling his wife; he didn't kill her, but she required medical attention. Two days later the twelve-month-old baby of the injured woman was found with strangle marks on its neck. The size of the finger impressions matched those of the baby's seven-year-old brother. This boy had witnessed his father strangling his mother. Perhaps he was imitating his dad; perhaps it was a coping mechanism as if he were trying to make sense of what his father had done. Whatever it was, the father had clearly provided the template for what could become an ongoing pattern of behavior.

A girl or boy living in a home where there is violence is not passively witnessing violence, as if he or she were watching it on TV. The child is experiencing that violence—and it has a huge impact on his or her developing brain. That child is a victim of violence. And although either boys or girls can go on to repeat the violence, boys are more likely to turn their horrifying childhood experience into a model for their own masculinity. To this we can add even more direct experiences of violence when that father or mother uses violence against that boy.

The Biggest Myth about Violence

One of the most common refrains we hear about violence is that it is natural. Part of the human makeup. In our genes. Unfortunate, but so are death and taxes. It's just the way it is.

You don't have to go back to Thomas Hobbes and his seventeenth-century declaration that violence is part of the "natural condition of mankind." These days, fanciful versions of this idea by some simplistic evolutionary biologists even proclaim that "moderate violence" is good for increasing human's "reproductive success."[12] Criminal violence, they add, is merely an unpleasant extreme of what, we're told, is actually good for us, sort of like the way a glass or two of wine is nice while a couple of bottles is going to give you a nasty headache.

Actually, there's some truth to the idea that violence is natural. As a species, humans certainly do have the capacity to be violent against other members of our species. Not all other animals have that particular talent. We do. That capacity is clearly in our biological makeup.

But the thing is, it's only a capacity. It's not a biological fiat as is, say, eating, drinking, or, from the viewpoint of the survival of our species, sex. How do we know? For starters, the majority of men (and women) don't exercise that capacity.

So, even if it is ultimately lodged in our biology, we need to ask, what turns a capacity into reality?

Research gives us one important clue. Anthropologist Peggy Sanday did some clever work a number of years ago.[13] She sifted through research from the past hundred or so years that looked at different tribal societies. This research gives us a window into our past, since many of these societies had been around for thousands of years, although many no longer exist or have now been irrevocably changed by the impact of dominant cultures.

Sanday examined the anthropological records with one question in mind: has there been violence against women, violence against children, and violence among men in all societies? The answer was clear. In about half the cultures, there indeed was violence. In the other half, there was little or no violence. This reaffirmed that violence is a human possibility, but also told us it was not an inevitability.

And what, she asked, was the difference between those societies with violence and those without? In each and every case, those with little or no violence were ones based on a high degree of equality. In contrast, those with violence were unequal ones based on male domination. These latter societies, patriarchal societies, were based on inequality, specifically the rule of men over women and the rule of some men over other men.

Does this mean that my half of the species is an irrevocably bad lot?

I like to think not. I think the real clue is not the word *male* in *male domination* but the words *domination* and *inequality*. As soon as you have societies based on some people having power over others and some enjoying the fruits of others' labors, you have the recipe for violence. After all, when push comes to shove, violence is the ultimate means of maintaining inequality. Think back to some of the most unequal of human societies: the slave systems of the southern United States and the Caribbean, or the apartheid regime in South Africa. In these cases, where a small number of people with light skin had power over the majority of women and men with darker skin, it was ultimately violence or the threat of violence that maintained that system.

I am not arguing that the situation of *most* women in the Americas or Europe or many parts of the world is as grim as people who are enslaved, although in some families in some countries it does come close.

But a simple truth remains. Male-dominated societies breed gender-based violence. But how does that filter down into one man and woman's relationship?

The Biggest Leap

Let me create a character, a man named Reg. He's not a real person, but a composite based on the conversations I've had with women staffing crisis lines or working in shelters for abused women, with men and women working in programs for men who use violence, with police officers and other first responders, and men I've met myself. He embodies what those on the front line hear every day, and he can help us explore why some men use violence in their relationships.[14]

If we could actually meet him, Reg might not seem like a nasty sort of man. He's friendly with folks at work. He goes to church. He gives generously to charity each year.

He also smacks around his wife—let's call her Sue-Ann. "Smack around" would be his words, not mine.

"Nothing too much," he says. "Except that one time when I kind of lost it."

When he gave her a black eye.

Bruised her chest.

Threatened that he was going to kill her.

When she thought he was going to kill her.

That time.

Although the big rules of the patriarchal game might be

decided in institutions—in places of worship, in parliaments, in courts, in corporate head offices—where most violence against women takes place is decidedly more personal and small scale. No law orders a man to hit his wife. No priest commanded him. His boss didn't tell him his job depended on it. So how do we make the leap from society as a whole to what this Reg does that day in the kitchen?

Men who commit acts of partner abuse tend to believe their relationship needs a boss and it should be them. This is an example of how the overall structure of a society gets reproduced throughout the society. It's kind of like the way a hologram works. A piece of holographic film has what looks like a senseless pattern of lines, but when lasers are beamed through it, they project a 3D image that hangs in space. One of the amazing things about holograms is that if you cut the film into small pieces, the lines on each small piece have the whole image on it. Throughout our society, any society, each little piece tends to reflect and reproduce the overall society (although sometimes in contradictory ways).

Men like Reg try to justify their actions. "I had a bad day. Everything goes tits-up. No time for lunch, nothing. Then I come home. Sue-Ann is supposed to get home before me and when I arrive dinner's supposed to be ready, I mean that's what we agreed, but this time she'd barely started. She had to visit some girlfriend of hers who has . . . some problem, but I'm thinking, who's more important here, me or this girlfriend? So I start yelling, and before you know it, well . . ."

One of the startling things about the stories I hear over

and over again is the sheer triviality of the excuses men use for their acts of violence and how they blame the person they have victimized.

Did my imaginary Reg really give her a black eye *because* dinner wasn't ready on time?

I'm guessing that men like Reg often find themselves waiting for something at work or in a long line at a store and don't go on a rampage. So why here, why now?

Part of the answer is that Reg was selectively using an act of violence to maintain power within his relationship. The punch wasn't about dinner. It was him asserting his authority, his right to be in control.

His act of violence is also about his sense of entitlement. Both Reg and Sue-Ann work outside the home. She normally gets home earlier and cooks dinner. But what makes him feel it's his right to have dinner waiting as if she were his servant? And, even worse, to punish her when his wishes aren't obeyed?

Since Reg isn't someone who most people would define as a violent person, it's clear he's selectively using violence against Sue-Ann as a tool for maintaining power and control over her.

To use the distinction I first heard from Marius Råkil, a Norwegian clinical psychologist, it wouldn't be accurate to describe this particular person as a violent man, but rather as a man who uses violence. In other words, the focus must be on his choices and his behavior.

This link between the use of violence by some men and social structures based on the uneven distribution of power between men and women formed the breakthrough insight in the 1970s and 1980s by feminist theorists and activists about men's violence. As Connie Guberman and Margie Wolfe wrote in 1985, feminists "discovered a social order, created and sustained by hundreds of generations that had institutionalized women's vulnerability and men's dominance in its social structures, laws, and attitudes."[15]

It's not enough to claim this man has an anger-management problem, or he is simply a violent man. We need to understand the systemic roots of the problem.

This is not to say that individual personalities, individual problems, even individual pathologies don't get into the mix, nor is it saying there are not some individuals who ooze violence from every pore, whom you'd definitely define as a violent man. But it is why feminists concluded that, ultimately, the solution to the problem lay not only in better laws (which they pushed for) but also in a world based on equality.

Men's role in bringing about such a world is key. If we want no woman to live in fear of this violence, men need to fight for equality throughout our institutions—economic, political, religious, cultural, and within the family—and support policies big and small that promote equality. For example, equal pay for women would contribute to ending men's violence: it means that power balances in relationships will be more equal and there is less chance that women will stick around abusive relationships because they feel they can't afford to leave. It also means that men have the job of challenging the power imbalances in our own lives. And even though men's role is key, it means supporting the women's rights organizations that will continue to be leaders in bringing about this change.

Cultures of Permission, Cultures of Rape

When I was a twelve-year-old in Durham, North Carolina, my fellow seventh-grade boys and I would gather under the sprawling pin oaks during recess and explain girls and sex. One day, a schoolmate gleefully explained the difference between "fucking" and "raping." It was simple, he said. Rape was "when you tied the girl to a tree." It was, apparently, the only way that he could conceive of any of us overpowering a female for, indeed, at this age many of the girls had started their growth spurts while we had not. The rest of us squealed with boyhood delight, both because we were talking about a taboo subject using words that, at the time, were seldom heard, but also because we saw it as a dirty joke.

Even if none of those boys went on to commit rape, for me it remains my earliest memory of what we now call "rape culture"—the trivialization of rape and the encouragement of attitudes and beliefs about both women *and* men that can lead to rape or blame the victim or make excuses for those who use violence.

Even if we boys didn't actually mean it in a literal way, when we repeated this explanation to each other or told hundreds of sexist and even violent "jokes," it was but one aspect of the permission our society has traditionally given to men's violence.

In many cases the permission is direct. Some men give

permission by direct example—as we saw above, boys who grow up experiencing violence in their own household are more likely to act in violent ways themselves. Far too often, these traumatized boys see that nothing is done about it. These boys grow up hearing their fathers' excuses and hearing their fathers blame their mothers for their actions. This can influence many boys who go on to be abusive themselves. This is permission by example from their father.

After one of my talks, a woman from the audience confided to me that many years earlier she had visited her priest to get help because her husband was beating her on a regular basis. The priest commiserated with her, but told her it was her duty to stay with her husband; it was the cross she had to bear. The priest was giving explicit permission to her husband's abuse.

Within the lifetime of most of my readers, as noted earlier, in many states it was legal for a man to rape his wife, a fact still true in many parts of the world. Even today, many states still treat it differently than other instances of rape—most egregiously in South Carolina, where a higher level of physical violence must be used, victims have only thirty days to report, and punishments are less severe.[16] This is permission and it is explicit.

The permission is explicit when we blame the woman who has experienced violence, when we say she asked for it because of the way she was dressed.

The permission is sometimes implicit. Men's violence against women is permitted if our predominantly male lawmakers don't pass effective laws to prevent it. (Because of the hard work of women activists, we can all be thankful that the legal situation has improved rapidly in many countries over the past two decades. In an increasing number of countries, we have some good laws concerning violence against women, although many can still be improved.)

But even if we have decent laws, they mean nothing if they're not skillfully, thoughtfully, and properly implemented. Until recently, when police officers went to a home where there was "a domestic," it was the common practice to simply caution both partners to "take it easy," as if it were a mutual problem. (I should add that many police officers whom I've met in recent years talk proudly of their current training and their mandate to treat these crimes as the violence that it is.)

Similarly, many women are still reluctant to go to police or even a hospital after they've been sexually assaulted, in part because their experiences with police, in courts, or even in hospitals have sometimes felt like being assaulted all over again. As a result of pressure from women's organizations, this is beginning to change with better training in some jurisdictions and specialized police and health units, but we still have a very long way to go.

The permission is also implicit when policy makers—again, predominantly male—do not see the importance of properly funding services that help women escape violence, training judges and prosecutors, or running public education prevention programs that spread the message that men's violence against women is illegal, immoral, and unacceptable.

And the permission is implicit when sexual harassment at the workplace isn't challenged. Again, we've made progress in developing workplace regulations to prevent or respond to sexual harassment, but effective training of staff and managers lags woefully behind.

But there's an even more pernicious form of permission.

"Just a Private Matter"

Imagine looking out the window and seeing a store being robbed. You would phone the police and tell them a crime was being committed.

And yet, every morning, women come to work with a black eye, or wearing a long-sleeve shirt on a hot day, or they miss work altogether because of injuries. No one reaches for the phone or even asks her if she needs help. Every night, neighbors hear women being threatened or beaten. No one reaches for the phone.

Every night, there are men who hear a friend boast how he's going to get a woman drunk out of her mind so she won't be in any state to say "no." Again, no one tells him he can't do that.

In all these cases, we say it's a private matter or a family matter.

Perhaps this is the biggest form of permission.

You might as well call it the male protection racket. It's a term I once saw on a clever poster featuring a photo of a group of male judges by the Scottish organization Zero Tolerance. And I should add, I know of the abuses of the justice system (by both male and female judges) but also many male and female judges who are champions of women's rights.

But it's not only males who buy into these ideas. Nor is it only males who come to think that the violence by some men against women is acceptable or, at least, unavoidable. For example, in a number of countries in eastern and central Africa, a large proportion of girls between four and twelve are genitally mutilated. The extent of this "genital cutting" varies from culture to culture; the United Nations estimates that between two and three million girls experience some form of this each year. Each year tens of thousands of girls die, millions suffer horribly through these procedures, and many women face lifelong health problems as well as a loss or at least a great reduction of sexual pleasure. In some communities it is thought of as an Islamic tradition (although it is not practiced in most Muslim countries); in a few, it's explained away as a Christian tradition, and in others it's called their tribal culture.

Whatever it is, though, it is arranged and, at least traditionally, largely performed by women. Women who went through this horror themselves. In this case it may not be violence by men against women, but these traditions persist because they've been defined as a way to (supposedly) please men. The supposed needs and desires of the dominant group dominate in each society.

What do these stories tell us about permission?

They do *not* tell us that women want to be beaten or raped or humiliated or mutilated. They do *not* tell us they ask for it.

However, they do tell us something about how cultures reproduce themselves. Once ideas are established, they become the accepted wisdom. The norm. In fact, girls and boys who grow up with these norms come to assume it's the only way things can be done. Although far more men than women have bought into the notion that violence against women is their right, it is true that some women have come to accept this as a horrible reality, in the way that you might accept that with life also comes illness, hardship, and death. Part of the importance of women's shelters as well as public education campaigns is that for some women and girls, for the first time in their lives, they learn it is a reality they do *not* have to accept.

What we can see from all this is that we can't only analyze the violent deeds of individuals. While it is true that individuals make choices, we usually do so within the boundaries set by our religions, cultures, laws, education systems, families, and community beliefs. As we've seen, for the past eight to ten thousand years, most humans have lived in male-dominated societies, ones where men have the power to shape the dominant ideas. Among those ideas has been the acceptance, to one extent or another and in one form or another, of violence by men against women.

Ending the permission of this violence is one of the most straightforward and important ways that men can make a difference. We need to do the following:

- Speak to any friends, family members, or co-workers who we think are being emotionally or physically abusive.
- Examine our own past and present attitudes and behavior.

- Find our own style and comfort zone to interrupt sexist jokes and sexist remarks—they're the background chatter of a culture that condones sexism and violence.

- Know that violence against women comes into our workplaces, especially in the form of sexual harassment. We all need to know company policies and ensure they're thoughtfully and effectively implemented where we work.

- Listen to and not trivialize women's concerns when it comes to their feelings about their safety and sexist language.

- Support better laws concerning violence against women and better funding for women's programs and antiviolence education. Support political candidates who say yes to these measures.

- Find ways to take action where we work, play, pray, or study. Encourage our ministers, rabbis, imams, and priests to speak out against this violence. Encourage coaches to talk to players on an ongoing basis.[17] Encourage activities in our kids' schools.

- Get active in awareness campaigns in our communities like White Ribbon, HeForShe, and many other fine efforts.

Toxic Paradox

The violence is about power and control. And it is about permission. But as we saw in chapter 3, there is a nasty paradox lodged in men's hearts and souls. The very ideals of manhood are impossible to live up to. The very ways we've constructed men's lives are the source of enormous uncertainty, isolation, and fear. This is intimately linked to the use of violence by far too many men.

Men deal with this paradox in different ways. Many realize it's a game they'll never win; they make peace with the fact that they'll never live up to the armor-plated ideals of manhood and just get on with their lives. But some men can't find that self-acceptance and instead develop different strategies to compensate or prove themselves or simply numb out. Some give themselves over to their job or to exercise; that is, activities that seem to help them live up to our expectations of manhood. Some men self-medicate with alcohol and other drugs. Some kill themselves—the suicide rate for men in the United States is more than three times higher than for women.[18]

And some use violence. They use violence as a tool to compensate for not feeling like a real man. Violence against other boys or men; violence against girls or women. Using violence restores, at least momentarily, his feeling that he is a real man.

Aggravating this is the insistence that men shouldn't show too many feelings or emotions. Emotions supposedly confer weakness and are deemed feminine. But think about it. We evolved as beings who constantly interact with other people and the world around us. A key medium of that interaction is a naturally rich emotional life. Emotions are a response to events and the actions and emotions of other people around us that trigger complex reactions by our autonomic nervous system. For example, in the face of imminent danger, we evolved to produce adrenaline, which pumps us with energy, temporarily reduces pain, and allows us to fight or run away. We evolved to react to hurt and sadness by crying. Our face tightens, tears flow, and afterward we feel better—and it's no surprise to discover that the tears you cry when you cut an onion actually have a different chemical composition than the tears you cry when you're sad.[19] When we feel great joy, we smile, our heart beats faster, and our levels of serotonin increase or, to put it differently, when certain things happen, serotonin levels increase and we feel happy.

But for men, tears or signs of fear are often seen as a weakness; unbridled joy is seen as too soft. Boys learn pretty early on to keep such emotions in check, and we get teased and humiliated if we don't. Our movies and sports culture celebrate the man who can take the pain—many tough-guy movies feature a guy getting beaten up or tortured but always able to resist giving in. So as boys, we actively work against displays of emotions; we work against even feeling certain emotions.

Sure, there are critical times when it's good to be able to keep emotions in check. I wouldn't want a paramedic breaking down in tears at the sight of an accident victim in immediate need of attention. The problem, though, is when the suppression of emotions becomes embedded into our whole being, when it becomes a way of life, and when we continue to be encouraged to suppress natural emotions even when the impact is terribly harmful. Rather than the natural and healthy experience of emotions, boys and men learn to lock them up tight. We become like a pressure cooker or a steam engine, and enormous energy can build up inside us.

And for some, a range of emotions gets transformed into an emotion we continue to reward in men: anger. The problem isn't anger; it's when we don't learn to express it in healthy ways. Even more so, the problem is when a vast range of emotions gets channeled into anger. In these cases, anger can explode in acts of physical and or emotional violence. You're stressed about work, freaked out about layoffs, feeling vulnerable. You're crushed by being out of work. You're belittled by being bossed around at work or by a society where others are given more power than you. You're torn apart because you're experiencing racism or living with abuse you suffered long ago. But real men are in control, right? Real men are the bosses. Real men don't get scared or feel vulnerable. But you can't just cry or ask for a hug. The feelings build up. They build up until they finally explode in the one emotion we give many men access to. And when anger isn't just felt but is exploding, it can easily get expressed as violence.

In other words, the violence that too many women experience isn't only because of men's power over women—and the way that some men use physical, emotional, and sexual violence to express and enforce that power. It's also because of the opposite: the unconscious feeling that a man has no power and, hence, he is not a man. And how can he compensate? How can he restore his masculine equilibrium? Violence becomes a tool to do just that.

This points to the critical importance of transforming the lives of men and boys. When we talk about men expressing feelings in healthy ways, it's not New Age mumbo jumbo. It's critical for ending men's violence against women, for ending men's violence against other men, for ending homophobia, and for improving men's health and well-being. In practice, this means we must do the following:

- Make sure we don't use humiliation to raise our sons. If phrases like *be a man* or *big boys don't cry* or *suck it up* pop out of our mouths, we better start digging deep to question why we are humiliating boys or other men.

- Support and encourage boys and men to be nurturing, not only in relation to their children or siblings, but also in our friendships and in the workplace.

- Challenge homophobia, which keeps boys and men conforming to narrow and harmful ideas of manhood and causes real hurt to LGBTQ people.

- Make sure the same rules and the same jobs apply at home and school to our sons and daughters.

- Don't make excuses for acts of violence or words of abuse, whether against women or men.

- Challenge sexist assumptions about men that come from both women and men. Challenge the poison of sexism and macho norms, whether in sports, politics, business, religion, or the media.

In other words, be equipped to take action wherever we can.

Fatherhood to the Rescue

Fatherhood is the final piece in the puzzle about men's use of violence.

Just as I believe that transforming fatherhood will prove to be the single greatest contribution by men to achieving gender equality, it may well be the thing that makes the biggest contribution to reducing men's violence—both against women and against other men.

I'm not only referring here to what I already said, that the biggest predictor of whether a man will use violence is whether he grew up in a home where the father acted in violent ways, either against the mother or against the kids. It's pretty obvious that loving fathers who never use violence against a spouse or children will help create a generation of boys (and girls) who are less likely to commit acts of violence.

That's true. But I'm also referring here to something subtler. Remember near the beginning of this chapter when I said that earlier societies based on gender equality had much less violence—against women, among men, or against children? And remember that in the fatherhood chapter I noted that in early, more equal societies, parenting work was more evenly shared? In a study of ninety-three tribal societies, sociologist Scott Coltrane discovered a strong link not only between fathers' active involvement and equality, but also with lower levels of violence.[20] The link between these points helps us uncover the final cause of men's violence and points to a key part of the solution.

What's the most important skill a parent needs in order to look after a baby or a toddler? Pretty simple: it's empathy, our ability to feel what others are feeling. You don't need a PhD in child development to understand why. Babies can't talk and toddlers have a limited ability to understand and express their emotions. Since they can't tell you when they're hungry, thirsty, tired, annoyed, frustrated, and confused, parents need empathy to sense the needs of the child and to respond in caring ways.

But here's the cool thing: the act of caring helps you develop empathy.[21] If from generation to generation, women are doing most of the caregiving, it means that women tend to develop more empathy than men. Empathy is part of the skill set that girls work at early on, practicing empathy with their dolls—*my baby's hungry, my baby's sad, my baby's tired.*

It's not that men have no empathy; of course we do. And of course there are some men with more empathy than some women. It's just that the ways we have traditionally raised sons combined with *who* does the raising means that men *tend* to have less empathy than we otherwise might have—empathy is a natural capacity, not a fixed quality.

For most men, our empathy is still in a serviceable or even strong range. But for some men it isn't. This seems particularly true for men who grew up in a home where there was a lot of violence against their mother. In such a home, some boys need to shut down their empathetic connection to their mom for their own emotional survival.

What is the link of this to violence? If you have reduced empathy, then you are more capable of committing an act of violence. You do not feel the pain you are causing. And so the man who hits his girlfriend says to police, "Oh come on, I barely touched her," although he broke her jaw. Another man says, "She wanted to have sex," when, in fact, she did not. These men are making excuses, but it's possible they believe their own words because they have limited their own capacity to feel what others feel.

Thus, if men are doing an equal amount of parenting work, then the boys who identify with them will hold on to their natural empathy and develop it further. And even though not all men become fathers, and even if circumstances prevent some men from being equally involved parents, empathy will become one of the markers of what defines a man. And if more men have more empathy, fewer men will be capable of hurting women, children, or, indeed, other men.

Just as men's relative absence from caregiving is one of the causes of men's violence against women, transforming fatherhood will reduce this violence and, thus, promote gender equality.

A Second Take: Empathy and the Bonds of Love

In the late 1970s and 1980s—ancient history, I suppose, for some—there were several books by feminist psychoanalysts and therapists such as Jessica Benjamin, Nancy Chodorow, and Dorothy Dinnerstein that touched on the impact of fathers' relative absence from parenting.[22] They weren't talking about bad or abusive fathers. They weren't talking about quality time with kids. They were simply looking at the impact of *quantity* time. Jessica Benjamin, in her book *The Bonds of Love*, said this: In a society where mothers do most of the care work—that is, they are the ones who feed, bathe, soothe, talk to, sing to, carry around, and are simply within eyesight of infants—for both boys and girls, the tie with the mother is the infant's first great bond of love. They are, psychologically, one with her. Remember our stick of celery? If the infant is the celery, first and foremost, that nurturing mom is the colored water they're drinking from. Meanwhile, if the father's role is a distant second, even if he is a sweet and loving guy, the infant will form a more distant attachment with him.

In their third year, infants begin to realize there are two sexes and begin to label themselves as one or the other. Although the understanding is still confused, they are getting fed a steady diet that is teaching them what we call a gender binary. You are supposed to be one or the other, male or female, masculine or feminine. For the boy, this presents a quandary. Not only is he supposed to be like this more distant person, his dad, but he's supposed to reject those parts of himself that he is now increasingly identifying with the mother. But in rejecting such things, he is rejecting his first great bond with another person. Instead, he begins to more strongly identify with someone he simply doesn't know in the same way. He is identifying, in a sense, with a fantasy object.

Two things are happening here. He starts developing a fantasy image of what a man is. And in a society where men have more power, it's no surprise that boys gravitate quickly to objects that, to their little minds, represent that power: trucks and cars, dinosaurs and superheroes, construction vehicles and guns.

The other thing that is happening, according to Benjamin, is that in order to cut off his first bond of love, the boy is erecting a strong ego barrier, a barrier between himself and others. Putting this into language that more of us are familiar with, he is setting up a limit to his experience of others, that is, to his own empathy. He is reducing his capacity to feel what others feel.

What is the result of that?

When fathers aren't equally doing the primary caregiving, infants develop a primary bond with the mother. And then, because we still draw a sharp line between males and females, the young boy needs to draw his own line. In rejecting femininity, in order to cast himself away from his mother, he needs to reduce his empathy and erect this barrier between himself and the world. And if he reduces his empathy, I believe he is more capable of committing an act of violence.

The transformation of fatherhood and, more specifically, men doing one-half of all care work will have a singular and long-term impact on ending men's violence against women.

Ending Men's Violence:
The Gender Equality Advantage for Men

It would be reason enough to work to end men's violence against women because of the appalling numbers of girls and women who directly experience such violence, because of the girls and boys exposed to and shaped by the violence in their homes, and because of the millions more women who live with the fear this could happen to them.

Yet the story of men's violence goes beyond this.

After all, as appalling as this violence is, it doesn't exist in isolation. For, just as patriarchy is a system of men's domination of women, it's also a system of power of some men over other men. As we've seen, violence or the threat of violence becomes a principal way to reenact, maintain, and extend that power.

I doubt there are many men who can't remember the name of the boy who threatened him or beat him up at school. Often there was an elaborate ritual surrounding these acts: the provocation and name-calling. The dares. And the fight that ensued if you rebuked the name-calling or accepted the dare. Or the beating that you got if you didn't fight back because you'd just confirmed you weren't a real man.

The study of young men's attitudes (conducted by Promundo) shows that 51 percent of men ages eighteen to thirty felt social pressure to use violence to get respect. Although only 23 percent actually agreed with that belief, that still represents one in four young men; I would guess the percentage would be much higher for those from ages ten to eighteen.[23]

And there is more. I doubt there are many men who don't still feel seduced by action movies—I know they still grab me in spite of myself. They're tales of (often male) protagonists who can inflict physical punishment while withstanding incredible levels of violence themselves. All without flinching, complaining, crying, or running away.

I know from the statistics that about one in eight men experienced violence in their childhood home. We used to call this "witnessing," as in the child saw or heard his mom being physically, sexually, or verbally abused. As I pointed out earlier, we know from the work of psychologists that these early moments are profound experiences of violence that can have a deep and lasting impact, especially if the violence was frequent, happened when they were very young, or was particularly severe.

We know from more and more men coming forward that far too many men experienced sexual violence as a child or young person, from unwanted touch to rape.

We know that gay, bisexual, and trans men experience particular threats of violence, in many cases from individuals but in some countries at an institutionalized state level. I don't just mean countries like Uganda, where gay men face death (in part because of successful lobbying efforts by US-based evangelical churches). I also mean countries like the United States, Canada, and England. It wasn't so long ago that the British computer pioneer Alan Turing was hounded to his death just shy of his forty-second birthday, seven years after helping the Allies defeat the Nazis. His crime was that he was a homosexual and was forced to choose between jail and chemical castration.

And there is the ongoing violence against men of color and indigenous men who experience heightened levels of violence.

In case you're missing a pattern here, it seems that many of these acts of violence by males against other males is either the ritualistic proclamation of one's masculinity, or a fantasy of men's heroism and power, or a means to "police" other boys and men to fit into the narrow definitions of manhood, or punishment for not being a member of the dominant group of men. In all of them, including sexual violence, we see a disregard for the impact of the violence; it has an almost casual quality, as if this is simply how it must be.

The causes of men's violence against other men are pretty much one and the same as men's violence against women. Acts of physical, verbal, or sexual violence are a means to reinforce lines of power. They are the result of some men having power over other men. They are paradoxically also the result of men *not* feeling powerful and needing to prove themselves as men. They are the result of boys and men learning to dull ourselves to the impact of pain on ourselves and others. They are the result of a sense of entitlement to have our way.

The violence hurts boys and men very, very deeply.

Men Campaigning to End
Men's Violence Against Women

One of the themes of this book is that we need to combine personal change with changes in laws, social policy, and the structures and institutions that not only are the remnants of eight thousand or so years of patriarchy but which serve to perpetuate that system. Institutions institutionalize things. Change isn't simply a matter of personal volition.

But how does change happen? There's a boring old debate: Do you change individuals, and then the collection of changed individuals means you have a changed society, or at least enough individuals who are pushing for a changed society? Or do you change the social structures in which we construct our individual identities and experiences? The answer, of course, is that both are needed—and life becomes a back-and-forth interaction between individuals and the broader world. This, however, begs the question of what creates the momentum of change.

Some people say that the existence of a problem in itself creates pressure for change. Perhaps so, but male-dominated societies have been around for millennia and, as far as we know, the first concerted challenge has come over the past century and a half and especially the last few decades (although there have long been female and male advocates for equality, and ancient Greece produced at least one play that was about women rising up against men). So if a problem isn't enough, what if there also is a widespread perception of a problem? That still isn't enough: to say the least, African Americans have always been aware of racism and discrimination, and there have been ongoing pockets of heroic resistance and solidarity, but again, it wasn't until the 1960s that a successful mass movement in the United States to challenge racism emerged—successful even though we still have a long way to go.[24]

I believe that what propels large-scale movements of change is not the mere existence of a problem nor even a widespread perception of a problem. It is when a solution is visible *and* when that solution seems achievable. Sometimes it is a small number of people who spark the flame, but it can spread into a wildfire only when a solution is widely visible and achievable.

What this means is a bit contradictory. An individual or small group of individuals can certainly play a key role. But their example will have an impact only if there is already a widespread experience of a problem and if, through increasing circles of concern and activism, it becomes apparent there is a solution to a problem and that solution is achievable.

It was a small group of women who got the ball rolling in the 1960s, but in spite of massive ridicule and resistance, their message immediately reverberated with the concerns of millions of others. Feminist ideas quickly spread across countries and around the world. As their ideas spread, more solutions presented themselves and, quickly, these solutions became attainable.

Meanwhile, among men and women working in organizations and communities to engage men in the change, the initial groundwork has been laid. I'm not saying moving forward will be easy or uninterrupted. But I am saying we now have evidence that large-scale involvement in support of gender equality and positive transformations in the lives of men is not only possible, but happening.

Men have an important leadership role to play in ending men's violence against women. As my colleague Jackson Katz says, "I don't believe that what we need is sensitivity training. We need leadership training, because, for example, when a professional coach or a manager of a baseball team or a football team . . . makes a sexist comment, makes a homophobic statement, makes a racist comment . . . some people will say, 'He needs sensitivity training.'. . . My argument is, he doesn't need sensitivity training. He needs leadership training, because he's being a bad leader, because in a society with gender diversity and sexual diversity and racial and ethnic diversity, you make those kind of comments, you're failing at your leadership."[25]

Ending Men's Silence to End Men's Violence

In chapter 1 I told the story of the White Ribbon Campaign. How two male colleagues and I, in 1991, horrified by the problem but also challenged by women to take action, started an effort that has spread around the world. What was unusual and important about White Ribbon was that it was the first time a mainstream effort focused on engaging boys and men on a women's rights/gender equality issue—not just as passive recipients of an implicitly feminist message but as actors for change. Much of our thinking was captured in our first slogan, *End men's silence to end men's violence.* We were encouraging boys and men to listen to the voices of girls and women and then forcefully speak out.

In most countries, White Ribbon focuses on education. Dates around November 25 (the UN's International Day for the Eradication of Violence Against Women) are often the focus, but in many places, it's a year-round effort. White Ribbon also works for changes in laws and government policies; some campaigns have specific programs in schools, workplaces, and the military.

One of the most unusual things about White Ribbon is that it's a decentralized campaign. From the start, we believed that men and women in their own nations and their own cultural communities knew best how to reach the men and boys around them. This approach has had both strengths and weaknesses. Because there was no ownership, it meant White Ribbon could spread beyond our wildest dreams. It meant that boys in a school or men in a community could take creative initiative to reach others around them. But it's also meant a total lack of organized communication or resource sharing—and much of the international connections have been ad hoc. This has limited its impact and prevented growth in other parts of the world.

In some countries or communities, there is an actual White Ribbon organization with a handful of staff members (or in the case of Australia, the world's largest campaign, a team of dozens) or a nongovernmental organization that makes White Ribbon an important part of its work (such as the Irish Men's Development Network, Gender and Society in Cambodia, Masculinity and Gender Equality in Chile, Instituto Papai and Promundo in Brazil, and Jane Doe Inc. in Massachusetts). Some campaigns are an annual effort run by an NGO, government body, service club, university, or business. In some countries it's just a symbol used by both women and men to represent ending violence against women—I once saw a postage stamp from Tunisia with a white ribbon on it.

We reach out to men across the social and political spectrum. While we will be critical of specific government policies concerning ending men's violence or keeping women in vulnerable or second-class positions, politically speaking White Ribbon is nonpartisan, because we believe that all parties must enact policies that work to end men's violence. And although there is a focus on reaching out to men, in many countries women are involved in the leadership of White Ribbon.

And we encourage other organizations and campaigns working to end men's violence against women to work in partnership with White Ribbon groups where they exist or simply to integrate the white ribbon into their own symbols or create their own cultural equivalent. One of my favorites is the Moose Hide Campaign, started by an Indigenous man and woman in western Canada, which uses a small strip of moose hide as a symbol of speaking out against men's violence.

Although I've referred to the white ribbon as a symbol, it's actually more than that. When a man wears a white ribbon on his shirt or around his wrist, sports a white ribbon T-shirt or hat, or puts up a poster in his office, he's doing more than supporting a cause. He's making a public promise not to commit, condone, or remain silent about violence against women.

Certainly there are men who get their backs up when White Ribbon and others raise these concerns. Some say we're accusing all men of being violent, which of course we aren't. Some men ask why we ignore the problem of violence against men. To that I reply that (a) we abhor all interpersonal violence, whoever commits it; (b) most violence against men is committed by other men, but if a woman commits an act of violence against a man that isn't in self-defense, then of course we condemn it; (c) when it comes to severe violence that sends someone to a doctor, that terrorizes them and leaves them living in fear, it is far more likely to be committed by a man against a woman than a woman against a man; and (d) every campaign needs a clear focus, and ours is helping end men's violence against women. Would anyone accuse an organization focusing on heart disease as being in favor of cancer?[26]

I like the story of White Ribbon because I'm proud I was able to play a role in developing and sustaining this initiative and seeing it spread so widely. And because it was the first attempt anywhere to develop a mass effort to speak to and actively involve hundreds of thousands and millions of men on a gender equality issue—and to prove it could be done.

But more than anything, when I think about the White Ribbon stories I hear from around the world, I'm constantly moved by the capacity of boys and men to step beyond our historic privileges and forms of power, to stand up to our brothers, to challenge ourselves, and to stand at the side of our sisters.[27]

And when it comes specifically to ending men's violence against women, once men add our voices to women's to call attention to the problem and to devote adequate laws and resources to ending it; once we ensure that we raise our sons with the knowledge that violence against women is unacceptable; and once we learn to speak out to our brothers, coworkers, teammates, and friends, then a number of very good things will happen: the dominant ideas of our society will shift with startling rapidity.

7

GENDER EQUALITY AND BEYOND

n the basement cafeteria, boys gave me shotgun glances. Tray in hand, I steered between the tables until two of them jumped up and bumped into me, one after the other. The first sent me off balance; the second sent me to the floor. The cafeteria went quiet, before erupting into cheers as if I had stumbled on my own.

It was 1963. I was twelve years old. Grade seven at Carr Junior High in Durham, North Carolina.

It is part of the story, the bedrock story, of my pathway to working for equality, social justice, and human rights.

Two and a half years earlier we had moved from Cleveland, Ohio, to Durham when my father accepted a position at Duke University Hospital and the Duke School of Medicine. It was a hard adjustment, for I had been pushed out of my protective childhood cocoon. I felt I was in a strange and foreign land, and by that I don't simply mean that everyone talked so differently. I mean that the South was still deep in racial segregation. Signs said which human beings could use this washroom or that water fountain. If I remember correctly, the politicians, the local baseball team, and the Duke basketball team were all white. From time to time the newspapers carried the story of a lynching or a cross burning.

My parents had clear rules in regards to segregation. We did not go to any restaurants that were segregated, which meant we almost never went out to eat. My sisters and I weren't allowed to go to a movie until the theaters were integrated, and so I watched wistfully as the other boys went to see war and cowboy movies. When I first protested, my parents said simply and clearly that as long as everyone doesn't get to do those things, then we don't do those things either.

During those years, in grades five and six and seven, I spoke out in the language of a child. Against segregation and, with respect for African Americans, using the then-respectful word *Negro*.

At the cafeteria at Carr Junior High, inmates that we were, we weren't allowed upstairs into the school until the bell rang. So I fled outside. The boys were right on my tail and quickly encircled me.

First came the ritual; they needed an exchange of words. Perhaps this was a relic from the days of gentlemanly duels. Or perhaps it was to disguise naked aggression, allowing the aggressor to pretend that he was required to use force to defend himself.

One boy said, "So you're a Yankee."

I still had a hard time thinking of myself as a Yankee,

which was a baseball team that had the nasty habit of winning the World Series.

"I'm from Cleveland."

There were laughs and taunts of "Cleveland" and "Yankee."

Another boy in the circle said, "And a nigger-lover."

"They're Negroes," I protested.

A third boy sneered, "And a Jew."

Jew thudded into me with two thousand years of force. Terrifying. Shame-inducing. Paralyzing.

Someone pushed me from behind and I stumbled across the circle, bumping into another boy. "Hey, he pushed me," he complained to his neighbor as he shoved me to the other side. Caught from behind, swirled around, this time pushed backward by a boy who spat the words "Dirty Jew." Across to a boy sneering "Yankee." Back and forth, spinning around, stumbling but never falling, the suffocating circle too tight, the chorus chanting, "Yankee, nigger-lover, Jew," and I was afraid to lash out to defend myself. Finally, the pack leader ended the lesson with a fist exploding into my solar plexus. I doubled over, unable to breathe, knowing for ten terrifying seconds I was going to die.

When my family moved to North Carolina, I wasn't prepared to be such an outsider, which is both the worst thing and the best thing that can happen to any child. The worst because children are natural conformists; to be separated out is to be stigmatized, which is to be humiliated. The best because it taught me, more than any political ideology could ever do, to identify with the have-nots and the oppressed. I got beat up with a tiny speck of the same hatred and tarred with one little bristle of the same brush as black people fighting for their freedom. And although my sufferings were puny in comparison, the punch of those bullies taught me in the gut that in some way I was on the same side as the oppressed.

Although these feelings of being an outsider had been brewing for the two years we'd been in the South, it was this moment, this punch, that guided me toward a lifelong path. What I mean is that I learned early on that I couldn't put myself outside the concerns of others even if I were living in my own protective bubble. I couldn't live in contentment if others were suffering, and I couldn't ignore the fact I was enjoying basic rights that others did not have.

That final punch was also a source of shame concerning my masculine credentials. Why hadn't I tried to fight back, hit back? Simply put, the mob of boys had terrified me. I was tinged with the awful feeling of not being a real man.

As we've seen, to some extent or another, all men carry some feelings, especially when we're young, of not living up to the demands of manhood. Some cope through displays of verbal or physical aggression. Most of us simply become very good at being one of the boys and doing what we need to do to prove we're a man. I certainly have done my share of that and, as they say, I can pass pretty well. So what gave me, and an increasing number of other men, the capacity to forge a somewhat different path?

For me, it was coming from such a secure and loving

family environment. It was being encouraged by my parents and by the religious tradition I was part of (postwar reform Judaism) to be a free thinker. It was the model of respect that my parents provided. And, a few years later, it was the emergence of the feminist movement and my friendships and loves with some amazing women who inspired me.

Gender equality is one of the great goals of our era. I've spent much of my adult life fighting for it.

But gender equality is not enough. I don't mean it isn't enough to satisfy all social shortcomings or make the world as perfect as we can make it—that much is obvious.

No, what I mean is that the many goals of feminism— transforming gender relations and our core experiences as women and men—require more than equality.

Often when we use the term *gender equality*, I believe it is really shorthand for deeper, wider, and more profound social change.

The Impact of Gender Equality

I don't recall ever hearing the term *gender equality* back in the 1960s or early '70s, although apparently it had popped up by 1971.[1] The new wave of feminism in the 1960s (so-called second-wave feminism, the first being the suffrage movement that won women the right to vote around the world) used the term *women's liberation*.

Even if now largely out of favor, *women's liberation* remains an interesting term because it captured two things the '60s were about: On the one hand, it was about personal transfor-

mation and personal liberation from the social and psychological fetters that hold people back. And on the other, the word *liberation* was very much in the air, from the liberation of Europe from Nazism only two decades earlier to the anticolonial, national liberation movements that were then sweeping Latin America, Africa, and Asia. Or, put in different terms, women's liberation embraced the notion that we needed both personal and social change and it needed to be much more than skin deep. Women weren't merely going to be equal to men but would be liberated, and the act of liberation would be theirs to lead. Moreover, achieving that required action at many levels; it required personal, interpersonal, cultural, political, and economic transformations.

I think we've lost something in losing the term *liberation*. I like the idea of human liberation.

On the other hand, a broader term than *women's liberation*—such as *feminism* or even *gender equality*—does suggest that men need to be part of the picture. That's a good thing.

But if our ultimate goal is only women's equality with men, we've got a big problem.

Let's imagine our world but with gender equality. We can say for certain that it would mean, by definition, women being equally valued in the economy, government, media and culture, religious and social life, and home. It would mean equal pay and that our institutions, from top to bottom, would have roughly equal numbers of women and men. It would mean women sharing equal authority with men in shaping public opinion and moral life. It would mean an end to job ghettoes where we find disproportionate numbers of

women or men. It would mean that men would do 50 percent of the care work. It would mean that whatever sex you were born (or choose to be) would have no bearing on your life's possibilities—except for some basic biological constraints.

Given that the economic and social power of men over women is the root cause (but not the only cause) of men's violence against women, gender equality will mean a great reduction of violence.

Gender equality will *probably* mean that the ways we raise boys and girls will continue to converge, at least to some extent. For example, we're already seeing a big increase in girls' participation in sports over the past few decades. Boy/girl differences in household jobs will continue to decline, mirroring changes among parents.

Beyond that, we can only speculate what gender equality *might* mean. For example, it might mean governments will put more resources into childcare and parental leave. Businesses and public-sector employers will more likely support family-friendly environments. Governments and religious institutions will be less likely to seek to control women's reproductive decisions. It might mean more caring societies, ones that find a more balanced relationship with the environment, ones that prioritize education and healthcare, ones that exploit people less. It might mean a different approach to politics and a lessening of international conflicts. It might mean less violence of all forms. It might mean that the gender binary, the rigid divisions between males and females, will be greatly reduced and headed for extinction.

Those possibilities are the type of things I hear over

and over about the results of gender equality. I hope they're true. But the problem is, there is no intrinsic reason they will come true. The assumption that equality automatically brings about all these positive results fails to recognize the complexity of the issues facing us; it ignores the intersectional nature of the problem. And it is also based on the false belief that females are intrinsically the opposite of males (or at least have significant and natural brain differences) and so equality would arithmetically bring into play the full panoply of human potential.

My earlier chapters make the distinction between biological sex (innate physical differences between males and females) and gender. I and many others have argued that many of the things we assume are male/female differences are not biologically fixed, but are the result of the different ways we raise boys and girls, different life possibilities and experiences, and different forms and experiences of social power. True, there may be some biological differences in male and female behavior, but I would argue that if so, (a) they are far less than we assume, and (b) they are only average differences, in the same way that, biologically, females are on average shorter than males and have less body hair and higher voices. The differences of such characteristics *among* males or among females is greater than the average difference *between* the sexes. I'd suggest that if there are average behavioral differences, they'd show a similar range and overlap.[2] And, finally, (c) I'd argue that we won't actually know the extent of innate male/female behavioral differences (if any)

until we've lived for many generations in a truly gender-equitable world.

There's a different way to approach the question of what difference gender equality will make. One is by looking at what currently happens when women are placed in the same positions men currently occupy.

I can't count the number of times that someone has told me about their awful woman boss. True, in some cases this is a sexist reaction to women's advancement. Or it's holding women leaders to different standards than we hold males to—what is seen as strong leadership in men gets trashed as bitchy or overly aggressive behavior in women. Or it might just be that this particular woman is simply a crappy boss. All those things can be true. But there is a fourth factor we seldom discuss. And that is, when someone becomes a leader, they do so within institutions, businesses, clubs, or structures that were shaped by centuries of male-dominated life.

Witness, for example, Margaret Thatcher, British prime minister from 1979 to 1990. Her "Iron Lady" nickname reflected a take-no-prisoners leadership style. Here was a woman leader who gutted social services (that disproportionately help women) and threw people out of work, both of which had a terrible impact on working-class families. She was a military hawk, showing no hesitation to order the torpedoing of an Argentinian ship during the Falklands War in 1982, killing more than three hundred people. She was one of the global architects of policies that began the process of concentrating most wealth into the hands of an increasingly tiny number of people.

I'm not criticizing Thatcher for not being warm and cuddly. But what I am saying is that she gives us the type of evidence that the issue in leadership is about power and whose interests you represent, not about what sex you happen to be.

I believe that it is critical that women equally inhabit leadership positions in all social, political, and economic institutions. This will bring new insights and skills to organizations and will mean that our institutions will look more like the people who work in them, their customers, and society as a whole. That's why I've fought for equal representation of women in politics, on boards, and in other leadership positions. But I know, as the Thatcher example shows, populating institutions created by men with women simply isn't enough.

Let me put this differently. In chapter 3 I looked at the costs to men caused by the ways we have defined manhood and men's power. If equality means only that women can occupy leadership positions and express power in the ways men traditionally have, then we have a problem, don't we? Yes, women should be able to do those things. But since my argument in this book is how such things have been paradoxically destructive to men (as well as women), why would anyone want women doing them too?

Do we all want more girls and women who can use violence to get their way? Indeed, when I talk to teachers, many say that violence committed by girls has increased markedly. Do we want women showing the same reckless abandon behind the wheel of a car that too many men have shown? Do we want girls and women ignoring their safety and health as a way of

showing how tough they are? Do we want women to assume that their job or career is, by definition, always more important than their relationships or nurturing those who depend on them? Just as I don't want such things for my son and grandson, I don't want them for my daughter and granddaughter.

The problem is, as chef and restaurateur Jen Agg says, it's not only male chefs who can be authoritarian jerks in the kitchen. "Women can be bros too."

In that sense, I'd say our goal can't just be gender equality, but rather a vision of human liberation outside of the narrow constraints created by eight thousand years of life in patriarchal societies.

A Dialogue on Gender Isn't Only about Male-Female Equality

Gender, as we've seen, is not only about women. It has to do with the ways we've constructed our identities and our lives as women and men or however we define ourselves.

One of the great contributions of feminism was to introduce a discussion that challenged the age-old assumption that biology was destiny.[3] It introduced a new language (for example, the distinction between biological sex and socially constructed gender) to make sense of women's lives. And by doing so, it's given us incredible new tools to think about the lives of men.

The theme of this book has been that men must do more than support women's rights—it also concerns thinking about and taking active steps to transform our lives as

men. When I see the enormous changes concerning fatherhood and when I speak to men around the world who are questioning the assumptions they were raised with, I see the powerful impact of feminism on men.

This has combined with the insights and challenges from LGBTQ peoples. They have bravely challenged our assumptions about the inevitability of heterosexual desire and fixed gender identities. In one of the great changes of our era, possibilities once forbidden and harshly punished are now, increasingly, being accepted as part of what makes us human. In all this, they have greatly enlarged the contours of a discussion around gender.

One aspect, for those of us men who want to fight for gender equality, is to realize the deep links between homophobia and our dominant ideas of manhood.[4] What keeps so many boys and men stuck in what many, following Paul Kivel, have called the Man Box? What keeps so many boys and men pursuing toxic forms of manhood that harm not only others but also themselves? Why is it so hard for many men to stand up to other men when faced with sexism or homophobia? Earlier I wrote that it is about fear of not being a "real man." Since none of us can live up to the demands of manhood, another way of saying that is that deep down we fear that other men will discover that we're not "real men" and we'll be punished for it. We certainly all had formative childhood experiences of that—being teased, bullied, or belittled for crying or showing supposed weakness or "acting like a girl." In other words, within our dominant ideas of manhood there is a fear of other men. Fear = *phobia*; men =

homo in Latin (although in Greek it means "same," hence fear of same-sex relationships). Homophobia is certainly fear or hatred based on someone's sexual orientation. But it's also a more generalized, although very deeply hidden, fear of other men. I believe that many of the institutions created by men, from bars to bleachers, parliaments to clubs, locker rooms to boardrooms, have a function of providing a space where men can feel safe together because we've worked out a set of explicit and implicit rules governing how we act with each other. One way many men have learned to act is to use sexism, homophobia, and in some cases racism (sometimes in the form of collective physical violence, sometimes in the form of jokes and insults) to bond together and negotiate our relations with each other.

Fear of other men becomes a constituent part of manhood. It's a mechanism for men to police themselves, to not challenge words and behaviors that we find objectionable. Furthermore, outright acts of homophobia—not only explicit insults or violence, but coaches teasing boys for "throwing like a girl," men playing golf who chide themselves with a woman's name if they don't hit a putt with enough force, taunts heard on the playground of "that's so gay"—are the daily verbal clutter of boys' and men's lives.

Taking it all one step forward, trans individuals or those who refuse all gender self-definitions push all of us further to question our most basic assumptions about gender and even biological sex.

So working to achieve gender equality really has dimensions that go beyond male-female equality. Once again,

we're drawn into a broader struggle for human liberation and justice.

The incredible news about this, despite the many challenges that lie ahead, is how quickly change is happening. I don't only mean at the official level, such as the advancement of same-sex marriage and adoption. I also mean at the individual level of personal experience. A couple of years ago I spoke to a recently graduated college rugby player. He and another straight buddy were going on a short trip together. They went to the car rental counter. The person asked if they were a couple. They asked why and were told that if so, they could both drive the car without paying a fee for the second driver. Without blinking an eye, they both said, "Of course we are." And when they got to their first motel, there was only one room left with a queen-size bed, which they shared without a second thought. The thumping homophobia that has too long been such a feature in the lives of men is thankfully starting to wear thin, although it still does incredible damage everywhere.

The result is not only important for gay, bi, and trans men. This is big stuff for all men. It means that all men have the possibility of closer relationships with other men without fear. With a reduction in homophobia, heterosexual men can have closer, more honest, and more affectionate relationships with other men.

Complicating Matters of Equality

Focusing predominantly on gender equality also ignores my earlier point, and the point made by many, that our expe-

riences aren't simply as abstract women and men. Rather, multiple parts of our experiences intersect to define us. As I pointed out earlier, my identity and practices as a man are shaped by being a straight, Jewish, middle-class intellectual type, an urban dweller, and a person with a US upbringing and a Canadian adult life. Those things are my own modifiers of manhood, and they help define what it is, for me, to be a man. These definitions aren't simply about identity; they are about complex constellations of power and privilege. For different people, different parts of their identity and experience are shaped most strongly if they are part of a group that is experiencing systemic discrimination or oppression. This is one reason why gender is a social experience: it is shaped through a range of interacting social factors.

For example, you can't for a second understand the life experiences or self-definitions of African American men without understanding the impact of slavery followed by a century and a half (and counting) of racism and discrimination, combined with struggles for equality, community-building, and self-expression. The high rates of incarceration, the large numbers of African American fathers not living with their children, the lower than average levels of higher education and income, or even the images of men and women in some hip-hop music are obviously not about being "men" in the abstract, but being African American men in a particular time and place. But it is also not about being "black" in the abstract but about being black *men*, as seen, for example, in higher levels of education and professional attainment among African

American women. These things work themselves out in complex ways.

One thing that this means is that even if we end the divisions based on sex—that is, for example, women come to occupy half of leadership positions or occupations—there would still be specific groups of women and men excluded from those positions based on other forms of discrimination and hierarchy.

That's why efforts to promote gender equality aren't isolated from struggles and initiatives to create fair and equitable societies overall.

To cite another example, recent years have seen the rapid acceleration of economic inequality. Today as I write, according to Credit Suisse, the 42 richest people in the world have the same wealth as 3.7 billion people (that is, half of humanity); the wealth of the richest 1 percent is more than the rest of the world combined.[5] And, since the ascendancy of the neoliberal policies and ideas celebrated by Ronald Reagan and Margaret Thatcher, we've endured decades of tax cuts that disproportionately benefit the wealthy and that inevitably lead to cuts in social and educational spending that would benefit us all. This has huge implications for the core issues I've been discussing. Say we're talking about transforming parenthood and relationships in the home. Sounds good. But working people, male or female, simply can't decide they want to be a more active parent if they are barely scraping by. They're going to be slogging in paid employment or gig jobs from early in the morning to late at night and spending hours on inadequate public transit rather than

spending time with their kids. The social, educational, and sports programs, the healthcare and affordable housing that are absolute requirements for a family-friendly economy and society, have suffered grievous injury. You might even conclude that if this trend continues, in a gender-equal society most men and women will be equal in *not* being able to prioritize care for children.

Meanwhile, as attacks on unions continue and as traditional industries scamper off to low-wage countries, as people are replaced by machines and more are working in underpaid service jobs or part-time or gig work, we're seeing more families under extreme economic strain. It's a recipe for an increase in violence against women in the home. And where will women escape to? In many jurisdictions, funding for women's shelters is being cut.

In other words, an agenda for meeting the promises and dreams that are assumed when we think about gender equality requires us to address a broader social and economic agenda.

Gender Equality, Patriarchy, and the Environment

One final note about why the promise of gender equality in the broadest sense requires us to set our sights even further. Humans now face the greatest existential threat of our two-million-year-long evolution: climate change.

As it turns out, climate change has a lot to do with patriarchy.

Remember the story I told in chapter 3 about visiting the

Paleolithic stones in Évora, Portugal? These were remnants of the early years of patriarchal cultures in that part of the world.

As they developed over time, male-dominated societies tended to be based on three forms of domination: Male domination over females. The domination of some men over others (based on ever-increasing social and economic divisions). And the domination of humans over nature.

Nature was increasingly seen as an external object to conquer. We, as humans, increasingly separated ourselves from nature's most harsh or deleterious effects and scorned as primitive those humans who still lived as part of nature.

The project of dominating nature was what allowed for rapid human ascendancy and spectacular and often quite wonderful scientific progress over the past eight thousand years.

But this very project also seems to be dooming us.

In previous eras, argues Ronald Wright in his brilliant *A Short History of Progress*, the negative impact of dominating nature was localized. Ever wonder why one of the cradles of civilization, the so-called Fertile Crescent—the lands of Egypt through Iraq—is now largely desert? In part it's because those earlier patriarchal societies got better and better, cleverer and cleverer at harnessing nature in order to farm. Eventually they sucked up most of the fresh water and eventually dried out and poisoned their land with salt. But this and other examples of what Wright calls "progress traps" were localized: humans slowly screwed things up and then moved on.

But now, in the course of only 150 years, humans have taken hundreds of millions of years of sequestered carbon (in the form of coal, peat, oil, and gas), burned it up, and spewed

vast amounts of carbon dioxide, methane, and other gases into the atmosphere.[6]

With this crisis, there is nowhere left to move.

In other words, talking simply about equality between women and men in what is being called the new Anthropocene epoch isn't enough to address the ravages of patriarchy.

Since patriarchy is a system based on the power of men over women, of some men over other men, *and* of humans over nature, then we all need to be part of an approach that allows us to undo the harm that patriarchy will continue to cause even if power and privilege is shared equally between men and women.

This doesn't mean turning our backs on science and technology. It doesn't mean rejecting the promise of new, beneficial technologies. But it certainly does mean rethinking who controls and who benefits from these technologies; it requires challenging our notion of progress and the supposed possibility of limitless growth.

This is part of understanding that gender equality in the narrow sense simply is not good enough. What is ultimately required is dismantling the edifice of patriarchy and building our future based on meeting the collective needs of humanity within a sustainable ecosystem.

Closing Words: Celebrating Men's Capacity to Fight for Gender Equality and Beyond

I was recently playing a round of golf with a man I hadn't met before. After a few holes he asked me what I did for a

living. I never quite know what to expect in these situations. He started with "that's interesting," and then as we walked along with our golf bags slung across our backs, I told him a bit more. He said, "Keep up the good work. I have four daughters." Another minute passed in silence until he came to a full stop. He turned to me and said, "Women just might save the world."

There was a time when I might hear such a comment at the site of an NGO project or on a march supporting women's rights, in a university classroom or a specialized conference. But these days, you don't have to travel far to discover boys and men who are embracing change.

One of the amazing things about the spread of this awareness is the number of men I meet who don't fall into the trap of being the gallant knight who thinks women need rescuing. Rather, they see their job as taking personal responsibility for supporting change. They realize that simply by being a man, they already have skin in the game.

Feminism and the massive push by women across the globe to achieve gender justice and women's rights represents the most fundamental, rapid, and widespread change in human history. In only fifty years, the world has watched as a tiny and marginal movement has blossomed into a force that touches every country, every institution, every religion, every workplace, and every family. Yes, in some places, advances have been swifter and deeper, but the changes are everywhere.

This revolution has certainly been a women's revolution. First and foremost concerning women and girls. First and

foremost led by women and girls. First and foremost embraced by women and girls.

And yet we are witnessing a spectacular change among those very ones who stand to gain from the status quo. Every single day, more and more boys and men are coming to grips with the negative impact of this status quo on the girls and women in their lives and the many they will never know. We are questioning our assumptions about what it means to be a man and are retooling our lives. True, this happens in sometimes fitful and uneven ways, but happen it does.

You and I are among the privileged generations who not only get to witness this most sweeping change in human history, we get to be part of it. It is a change that your descendants will still be talking about in a thousand years.

For men, this is it. This is your chance to join women in making history. This is your chance to undo past wrongs. This is your chance to create a better world for women but also for men. This is your chance to transform workplaces and institutions and to end laws and beliefs that have done so much harm to women. Ones that, in paradoxical ways, have not only brought forms of power and privilege to boys and men, but have been destructive to men ourselves. This is your chance to help ensure that our children and grandchildren have possibilities and lives free of the narrow constraints that have too long endured.

The time has come for men to join the gender equality revolution.

AN ACTION GUIDE TO ENGAGE MEN

The chapters in this book explore specific areas where women's and men's lives are rapidly changing, and where men can play a critical role in supporting gender equality and bring about positive changes in their own lives.

From the work I've been doing over the years and from evaluations of projects developed by my colleagues across the country and around the world, we now have a strong evidence base to know what works and what does not when it comes to engaging the men and boys around us.

Here are some core points for men who want to be part of the gender equality revolution, and for those women and organizations—businesses and unions, government departments and schools, religious institutions and nongovernmental organizations, police departments and sports leagues—that want to engage boys and men to support gender equality.

Positive messages score. Although it can be tempting to berate our fellow men for their shortcomings, it's simply not an effective way to connect with others. Our goal is not to show how much more enlightened we are. It's to affect change. So, for example, if I say, "Why aren't you doing anything in your company to make sure women have equal opportunities?" most men will get their backs up. They'll protest that they *are* doing things. End of conversation. But if I start the conversation differently, it's going to open up a dialogue and create a space for a man to think about what he can do: "Why not take the opportunity to make more of a difference in your company?" or "This is an important time for men like you to be speaking out to support gender equality and end violence against women" or "I'm guessing you know these are important issues, so maybe I can help you figure out some steps you can take to make a difference."

Gender-transformative approaches. Keep in mind the paradox of men's power. Patriarchal societies give men a leg up. But the ways we've constructed this privilege and power come with big costs to men ourselves. What this means is that boys and men will more likely support change if they feel it will also transform their own lives in positive ways. And so, a theme of our work must be to transform the ideas, ideals, and practices we attach to manhood . . . True, you and I might wish that every man supported gender equality even if it meant losing out. But the simple fact is that many men will either oppose change if they think they stand to lose,

or at best stand on the sidelines and think these issues have nothing to do with them.

This point is particularly interesting. We know that boys and men carry a lot of unconscious fears about not being "real men." So you would think approaches that challenge our ideals of manhood wouldn't get far. But, in fact, by doing so, we can connect with truths that men feel deep down—that they can't ever live up to the destructive ideals of manhood—so challenge these ideals we must.

This becomes a powerful tool for promoting engagement and change.

Broad-based unity and working respectfully through differences. Creating a society of gender justice and healthier lives for women and men won't be achieved if those who support change remain a minority. Sure, a minority can start powerful movements of change. But a minority can't finish the job. That happens when solid majorities are mobilized for change—in our workplaces, communities, schools, places of worship, homes, and governments. Our efforts must be as practical as possible and must attempt to connect with as wide a swath of the population as possible. Our job isn't to feel superior or different than others; it's to connect with others. That requires going to where people are—both literally (in the sense of going to where they work, shop, pray, and live) and figuratively (in the sense of finding language that truly connects with them.)

This means ensuring that the issues of gender equality become completely mainstream. If you believe in equality,

then you must believe that everyone should hold those ideals. That, by definition, is going mainstream.

Achieving this requires working in partnerships with people you might disagree with on many other issues. I might disagree with someone on, say, the impact of climate change or who we vote for; I might even detest who they vote for. But if we agree, for example, that we need high-quality childcare as part of our public education system or that their girlfriend, wife, or daughter should get paid equally to men, then I'm going to find ways to work with that person.

That doesn't mean ignoring the fact we have differences on important issues. It means agreeing to disagree on those things and working together with respect in spite of those differences. Meanwhile, we can continue to speak out on the things we believe in and keep making the connections between feminism and a range of issues critical to our times.

Challenge sexism. Creating broad-based unity, being positive, and going mainstream, though, can be tricky business. For one thing, it doesn't mean ignoring sexist assumptions, words, or behavior. It's critical that men learn to speak out when our workmates or friends act badly. The point is, when possible, to challenge sexism in ways that connect and bring about change.

Reach out to boys and men with compassion and empathy. We might be totally offended by the words or actions of a man. But since reaching them with our message and affecting change is our goal, we need to understand the root of

their feelings and actions. This is not to ignore or excuse sexist or abusive behavior. But it means we always need to figure out where people are coming from. For that, listening and asking questions are key.

Ongoing, steady work is needed. One-shot approaches won't do the job. Many organizations and communities support special days (International Women's Day, initiatives linked to Father's or Mother's Day, White Ribbon Day, the progressive TV ad shown once a year, and so on) as their sole moment for focusing on gender equality issues. Similarly, many companies figure they can check off a box with little effort. For example, somehow they believe that handing someone a policy sheet or having them do a twenty-minute online "training" will be sufficient to prevent sexual harassment at the workplace.

True, a one-shot approach is usually better than nothing. However, both common sense and the evidence base shows that this doesn't get the job done and, worse, it can create a false illusion that you've taken effective action. Ongoing efforts needn't be nonstop. But messages need repeating; we need creative and varying approaches in the course of the year. And in the workplace, training of staff can't happen just once, and managers and supervisors need ongoing support to make a difference.

Listen to the voices of women; build partnerships with women. The focus of this book and the efforts it advocates may be focused on men, but any work we do must be in

partnership with and with respect for the women around us. In a way, outreach to men starts by listening to the voices of women and with support for women's leadership. You want to work in your company to promote gender equality? The best way to find out where to start is by following the lead of your women colleagues. Meanwhile, in our communities and across the land, there is huge reservoir of knowledge within women's organizations. Going beyond listening and actually building partnerships can be challenging. But no one said changing eight-thousand-year-old social structures, relations of power, and cultural practices was going to be easy.

Make it personal. It's no good if I as a man wave the banner of women's rights and then go home and expect the little woman to cook and clean for me—or worse, if I'm emotionally abusive. Holding ourselves and our fellow men accountable for our actions is critical. But accountability and making it personal doesn't mean I'm rushing out to buy sackcloth and ashes. Accountability does not equal self-flagellation. Rather, it's about working hard to create positive ideals of manhood.

Understand there's not one experience of being a man. Challenging men's privileges in a male-dominated world requires nuance for the simple reason that patriarchy is not only a system of men's collective and individual power over women, but the power of some men over other men. For a movement of men to be an inclusive and diverse movement of men, we need to appreciate our very diverse rela-

tionships to patriarchal power. The man scraping by with two minimum-wage jobs that keep him working morning, noon, and night has a very different relationship to men's power than a man sitting comfortably in the middle or upper reaches of economic, social, or political power. The man, rich or poor, who is born with a leg up simply because his skin is white or he speaks English without an accent or he is heterosexual enjoys forms of privilege, acceptance, and personal safety that many men do not. We must be aware of these differences in men's lives and the complex equation of power and then work to end all forms of discrimination, oppression, and inequality that separate rather than unite us. But, to turn it around, it also means that our cultural and other differences bring a wider range of possibilities and experiences that can help enlighten our collective futures.

Combine personal change with broader social change. We have a tendency, especially in North America, to assume that the alpha and omega of change is personal. If I say, "transform fatherhood," many will hear that as a message that men should take on half the caretaking work in the home or, at least, spend more time with the kids. That's well and good. But change isn't simply about individual action. It's about making the social changes that allow and encourage individual change. The development of social and economic policies at a local, state, and national scale (and the tax base that will support those policies) and policies within our individual companies will help set the stage and provide opportunities for individual change. And individual change, in turn, cre-

ates demand for more social, political, and economic change at the macro level. That's why the prescriptions in this book include suggestions both for individual action and change, and for the types of social and corporate policies we need.

Create safety for men. You would think, wouldn't you, that if you had a few thousand years to create societies where your half of the species ran the show, you'd create a society where you felt awfully safe. But because our ideals of manhood are impossible for any man to fully live up to, men often don't feel safe as men. Many men don't speak out against sexism or homophobia or about their mental or physical health issues because they worry about what their buddies will think.

That's why men's leadership is particularly important. When men, especially those in positions of leadership, take a stand in both words and deeds, it creates safety for other men to do the same.

Leadership comes in many different forms. There are elected leaders in government, schools, professional associations, and trade unions. Appointed leaders in business and the military. Leaders in the office or on the shop floor. Opinion leaders in the media or the barbershop or the bar. Leaders on the sports field.

Leadership by men isn't to replace but to complement women's leadership.

It's to visibly show that as men, we *must* speak out, and we *can* speak out.

And that's why throughout this book, I've talked about men's leadership for change.

COULD WORK TO ENGAGE MEN BE AGAINST WOMEN'S INTERESTS?

Over the years, some women's and feminist organizations have occasionally voiced a concern about valuable resources going "to men" rather than the women's organizations that are desperate for funding. They rightfully worry that efforts to reach out to men and boys could carve off a big slice of the funding pie. But I feel that by engaging men, we will actually address this concern. First of all, men still control the budgets of governments and organizations. As men develop a deeper awareness of and connection to these issues, more funding will go toward women's efforts. As one colleague puts it, rather than argue about how to split up the pie, let's bake a bigger one.

Engaging men is part of the solution to the problem. As more and more men (who are still disproportionately the lawmakers, police, judges, and opinion makers in the media, in religion, in the locker room, and on the street) speak out

to end men's violence against women, for example, more of those men engaging in abusive behavior will be challenged and more good laws will get passed and implemented.

Moreover, it's men who have the greatest influence on boys or other men over how they define themselves as men. So if men say nothing or do nothing about the violence, or if men don't speak to a fellow soldier or fellow student or fellow executive who is about to commit sexual assault, or if men don't speak out if a friend is belittling his wife, then the violence will continue. With men's strong involvement, men who use violence will increasingly realize that other men do not accept their actions. More boys will learn from the start that violence is not compatible with healthy relationships or our ideals of manhood. More male workplace managers will learn to take action to end harassment.

In other words, although efforts to engage men require money to be spent "on" males, the goal here is to meet the needs of women and girls. It is to achieve women's rights, as well as promote the social changes that will benefit both females and males and, indeed, those who do not define themselves in either way.

If men do hear such concerns about scarce resources, let's listen with respect and then figure out how to thoughtfully address them. I remember back in the 1990s, there were even rumors that the cofounders of White Ribbon were receiving lavish salaries when, actually, not only were we volunteers but at one point my cofounder, Jack Layton, had put up his house, and I'd put up my car to guarantee a loan so we could print posters and educational materials and reach

out to Canadian men. We did our best to correct the rumors but, in the end, we decided the best response was just to get on with our efforts.

Although in the 1990s and 2000s, I frequently heard these concerns (that work with men and boys takes away resources or attention from women and girls), they are less frequent now. In fact, I'm more likely to hear, "What took you so long to join us?" At the same time, women rightly say that men's efforts must be informed by and be accountable to women's organizations in our communities. Which is one reason why the networks I'm part of, White Ribbon, the MenEngage Alliance, the MenCare Network, and Promundo (the research and programming organization where I am a senior fellow), have close ties with UN agencies including UN Women and the United Nations Population Fund and work closely with international, national, and local women's organizations.

RED LIGHT, GREEN LIGHT

A Fresh Approach to End Workplace Harassment

n the face of concerns about sexual harassment and inappropriate behavior in the workplace, what's a man to do? How are managers supposed to respond? Must men tiptoe around our workplaces? I now hear some men saying, "I never tell a joke at work for fear of offending someone," or "I never touch a woman except for a quick handshake," or "I never have a coffee or travel for work with a woman unless others are present." I even had one man (who had been found responsible for sexual harassment) tell me, "Nowadays, I keep my eyes down in the elevator. I get off and walk to my desk without looking at anyone."

I don't know about you, but I don't want to be in a workplace where no one jokes, no one smiles, no one compliments anyone or asks how they're doing.

Being counted in as a man personally committed to workplaces free of harassment has its challenges, but it's not

as hard as some think. First of all, don't be paranoid. It's not as if women are going to light up the Bat Signal to call in the Politically Correct Police if you utter the slightest wrong word.

Second, we can benefit from a "should know" criteria. I should know that certain behaviors or words are never appropriate in the workplace. Or I should know that they're not appropriate for someone in my position—there are things that might be fine with friends or even workmates, but not if I'm a supervisor.

But what about all those things in the gray area? I often hear many men say, "How am I supposed to know?"

That's where training, empathy, and listening come in. If I do something as innocuous as pat a woman or a man on the shoulder and sense them flinching, or if, when we next meet, they stand a bit farther away, then for me that is a clear sign my action made them feel uncomfortable. It is a message that what I meant as a friendly pat is making her or him uncomfortable. In other words, as I talked about in chapter 4, harassment and inappropriate workplace behavior often aren't about intent but impact.

The approach I've taken in my own consulting and training work with the United Nations, companies, educational settings, and the public sector to grapple with workplace harassment is what I call the Red Light, Green Light framework. Think of a traffic signal. Red and green don't usually get people in trouble. If you're paying attention, you know exactly what to do. Stop or go. Where we get in trouble (and when accidents often occur) is with the yellow light. It's a

warning light. It tells you "proceed with caution" or "be prepared to stop."

There are some types of workplace behavior that are always inappropriate. Using certain racist or homophobic or sexist words. Making clearly degrading comments about a certain group based on sex or race, gender identity or religion, and so forth. Pushing someone you supervise to have sex. Posting porn. Think of things like that as a red light. Even if some others at your workplace say or do those things, always stop if you hear yourself doing that. And find effective ways to tell others to do the same.

Then there are things that are always appropriate. You can be friendly to coworkers. You can put up a family photo or pictures of your kids. You can have a coffee or lunch with coworkers if both of you want to do so. The list could go on and on. Think of these behaviors as a green light.

But as we saw in chapter 4, there is a long list of behaviors that aren't clearly red light or green light. Touch someone? Compliment them on their looks or clothing? Tell a joke? Flirt? Are such behaviors appropriate? Could they ever constitute harassment? The answer is, it depends. So think of these as the yellow light, the warning light. Sure, do these things if you're pretty sure they're appropriate, but know the caution light is flashing. And just as when your car enters an intersection as the light turns yellow, go on high alert. You're instantly watching out for others; you're seeing how the car behind you is reacting, you're looking out for oncoming traffic.

Same thing with workplace behaviors in the yellow zone.

Sense the impact it is having on the person the action or comment is addressing and on others present. How will others in the workplace who'll hear about it interpret it? And if you know that yellow has turned to red, put on the brakes and, if appropriate, apologize.

This red light, green light approach respects people's intelligence—in fact it's a simple tool to build workplace emotional intelligence. It gets us away from simplistic lists of dos and don'ts. It's a nice counterpoint to overly rigid and unenforceable policies. And it gives managers a tool to intervene in low-level inappropriate behavior without calling out the National Guard.

Acknowledgments

There are so many feminist women and pro-feminist men I've worked with, learned from, and admired over the years—a few are names in the news but most are the scholars and local activists, the teachers and service providers, the organization builders and the convention shakers who are changing the world.

Thank you to my colleagues at Promundo, especially those who gave me feedback, provided references, or answered questions during the writing of this book: Giovanna Lauro, Ruti Levtov, Alexa Hassink, Brian Hellman, Nikki Van Der Haag, and Gary Barker.

Let me give a shout-out to the many scholars now studying men and masculinities, and to activists working to engage men to promote gender justice as well as better lives for men, with a special nod to colleagues in White Ribbon campaigns around the world, those in the MenCare and

MenEngage networks, and Dean Peacock at Sonke Gender Justice in South Africa and Rob Okun at VoiceMale. For their help in many different ways, thank you to Manisha Aggarwal Schifellite, Rebecca Ladbury, Gord Cleveland, Sue Colley, Goli Rezai-Rashti, Marie-Lynn Hammond, Philip Hebert, Maggie Baxter, and Michael Kimmel. And I want to particularly acknowledge my late friend, coauthor, and scholar Harry Brod, a Jewish man born in Berlin after the Holocaust who was the kindest and most thoughtful teacher of them all.

Thanks to the many people I interviewed or reached out to for advice, and to those I've spoken to during my travels who have enriched my understanding with their insights and stories. A few who I interviewed or consulted for this book are mentioned by name in these pages; others who I interviewed about their experiences are there by first name only, and many others were critical to my own thinking even if they aren't referred to or quoted directly. I thank you all.

To my literary agent, Julia Lord, for her many insights that helped shape this book, for her hard work all along the way, and especially for her commitment to social justice.

To my editor at Counterpoint Press, Dan Smetanka, for his wisdom, critical eye, energy, and humor, and to the whole production, marketing, and publicity teams at Counterpoint Press, Brilliance Audio, and House of Anansi Press.

The bedrock for everything I write about and the path I've followed lies with my parents, Rita and Nathan—now both gone. Indeed, this is the first of my books that my father, who lived to almost 101, didn't read and comment on

before publication. And thanks to the love and support of my sisters Naomi, Miriam, Hannah, and Judith—you're all my favorites—and to their spouses Steve Price, Roberta Benson, Mary Murphy, and Neil Ironside, and also to Lisa Alexander for their good cheer in the face of a formidable family. And with the greatest of affection for Nathan and Gwen who remind me of everything that one should know.

To my son Liam Kaufman and my stepdaughter Chloe Hung—sources of constant joy, of delight at their accomplishments—but mainly for their sheer goodness, for their help answering arcane questions, and for the things they both continue to teach me about myself and the world.

And as always to Betty Chee for her ongoing encouragement, sheer toughness in the face of sexism and racism, smart humor, and never-ending devil's advocate challenges.

Endnotes

1: The Time Has Come

1. Michael Kaufman, *Beyond Patriarchy: Essays by Men on Pleasure, Power, and Change* (Toronto: Oxford University Press, 1987).
2. Jack's and Ron's partners were, respectively, Olivia Chow and Jan Peltier.
3. The twenty-one members of the G7 Gender Equality Advisory Council (from Canada, Denmark, France, Germany, Japan, Italy, Liberia, Pakistan, South Africa, Uganda, United Kingdom, and the United States) were Dillon Black, Emma Bonino, Winnie Byanyima, Diane Elson, Rosemary Ganley, Melinda Gates, Leymah Gbowee, Dayle Haddon, Yoko Hayashi, Isabelle Hudon, Katja Iversen, Roberta Jamieson, Michael Kaufman, Farrah Khan, Isabelle Kocher, Christine Lagarde, Phumzile Mlambo-Ngcuka, Maya Roy, Isabell Welpe, Christine Whitecross, and Malala Yousafzai.

2: Listening to the Voices of Women

1. When I identify someone by their first name only, it is either a name I've assigned to them or, in cases when interviewees gave permission, their actual first name.

2. Peggy McIntosh, "White Privilege: Unpacking the Invisible Knapsack," in *Understanding Prejudice and Discrimination*, ed. S. Plous (New York: McGraw-Hill, 2003), 191–96.

3: Men's Lives in a Male-Dominated World

1. There are so many books now on how we have raised boys to be men and how we can do it much better. See, for example, Michael C. Reichert, *How to Raise a Boy: The Power of Connection to Build Good Men* (New York: TarcherPerigee, 2019); Judy Chu, *When Boys Become Boys: Development, Relationships, and Masculinity* (New York: NYU Press, 2014); William Pollack, *Real Boys: Rescuing Our Sons from the Myths of Boyhood* (New York: Random House, 1998); Niobe Way, *Deep Secrets: Boys' Friendships and the Crisis of Connection* (Cambridge: Harvard University Press, 2011); Gary T. Barker, *Dying to Be Men: Youth, Masculinity and Social Exclusion* (New York: Taylor & Francis, 2005); Dan Kindlon and Michael Thompson, *Raising Cain: Protecting the Emotional Life of Boys* (New York: Ballantine, 2000); Daniel J. Siegel, *Parenting from the Inside Out: How a Deeper Self-Understanding Can Help You Raise Children* (New York: TarcherPerigee, 2013); Peg Tyre, *The Trouble with Boys* (New York: Harmony, 2009); Geoffrey Canada, *Reaching Up for Manhood: Transforming the Lives of Boys in America* (Boston: Beacon Press, 1998); and Olga Silverstein and Beth Rashbaum, *The Courage to Raise Good Men: You Don't Have to Sever the Bond with Your Son to Help Him Become a Man* (New York: Penguin Books, 1995).

2. For a scholarly review of experiments like this, see Marilyn Stern and Katherine Hildebrandt Karraker, "Sex Stereotyping of Infants: A Review of Gender Labeling Studies," *Sex Roles*, 20, nos. 9/10 (January 1989): 501–22.

3. See, for example, Lise Eliot, *Pink Brain, Blue Brain: How Small Differences Grow into Troublesome Gaps—and What We Can Do about It* (Boston: Houghton Mifflin Harcourt, 2009).

4. R. W. Connell, *Masculinities* (Berkeley: University of California Press, 1995).

5. Varda Burstyn, *The Rites of Men: Manhood, Politics, and the Culture*

of Sport (Toronto: University of Toronto Press, 1999); Michael A. Messner, *Power at Play: Sport and the Problem of Masculinity* (Boston: Beacon Press, 1991); Michael S. Kimmel, *The History of Men: Essays on the History of American and British Masculinities* (New York: State University of New York Press, 2005); Bruce Kidd, "Sports and Masculinity," in *Beyond Patriarchy: Essays by Men on Pleasure, Power and Change,* ed. Michael Kaufman (Toronto: Oxford University Press, 1987), 250–65. And for a short popular account of this, but also on pathbreaking efforts to change sport culture, see MenEngage-UNFPA Advocacy Brief, "Sports and the Making of Men: Transforming Gender Norms on the Playing Field" (Washington, D.C.: Promundo, United Nations Population Fund, Sonke Gender Justice, MenEngage, 2013), www.promundoglobal.org/resources/sports-and -the-making-of-men-transforming-gender-norms-on-the -playing-field.

6. Mary O'Brien, *The Politics of Reproduction* (London: Routledge and Kegan Paul, 1981).

7. Norman Doidge, *The Brain That Changes Itself* (New York: Viking Penguin, 2007).

8. I explored the paradox of men's power in my book *Cracking the Armour: Power, Pain, and the Lives of Men* (Toronto: Viking Books, 1991).

9. Ellen Galinsky, Kerstin Aumann, and James T. Bond, *Times Are Changing: Gender and Generation at Work and at Home in the USA* (New York: Family and Work Institute, 2009), 10, familiesandwork .org/downloads/TimesAreChanging.pdf.

10. Brian Heilman, Gary Barker, and Alexander Harrison, *The Man Box: A Study on Being a Young Man in the US, UK, and Mexico* (Washington, D.C., and London: Promundo-US and Unilever, 2017), 28.

4: The New 9 to 5

1. Bureau of Labor Statistics, *Current Population Survey 2016,* US Department of Labor, https://www.bls.gov/cps/cpsaat08.pdf.

2. European Institute for Gender Equality, *Europe Gender Equality Index 2015. Measuring Gender Equality in the European Union 2005– 2015* (Vilnius, Lithuania: EIGE, 2015), 29.

3. US Census Bureau, *Current Population Survey 2017 Annual Social and Economic Supplement*, www.census.gov/library/publications/2017/demo/p60-259.html.

4. McKinsey Global Institute, *The Power of Parity: How Advancing Women's Equality Can Add $12 Trillion to Global Growth* (September 2015).

5. Bureau of Labor Statistics, *Current Population Survey 2016*, US Department of Labor, www.bls.gov/opub/reports/womens-earnings/2015/pdf/home.pdf.

  Canada: www.statcan.gc.ca/pub/89-503-x/2015001/article/14694-eng.htm.

  Europe: Eurostat, "Women in the EU Earned on Average 16% Less than Men in 2016" (March 2018), ec.europa.eu/eurostat/documents/2995521/8718272/3-07032018-BP-EN.pdf/fb402341-e7fd-42b8-a7cc-4e33587d79aa.

  Japan: asia.nikkei.com/Politics-Economy/Economy/Japan-s-gender-wage-gap-persists-despite-progress.

6. Deloitte, "Technology, Career Pathways and the Gender Pay Gap," www2.deloitte.com/uk/en/pages/growth/articles/technology-career-pathways-gender-pay-gap.htm.

7. US Dept of Labor Statistics, *Current Population Survey, 2014 Annual Averages*, www.dol.gov/wb/stats/latest_annual_data.htm.

8. Elise Gould and Teresa Kroeger, "Straight out of College, Women Make About $3 Less Per Hour Than Men," Economic Policy Institute (June 1, 2017), www.epi.org/publication/straight-out-of-college-women-make-about-3-less-per-hour-than-men.

9. McKinsey & Company and Lean In, *Women in the Workplace 2016*.

10. Corinne A. Moss-Racusin et al, "Science faculty's subtle gender biases favor male students," *Proceedings of the National Academy of Sciences of the Unites States of America*, vol. 109, no. 41 (2012), www.pnas.org/content/109/41/16474.full.

11. Claire Cain Miller, "It's Not Just Mike Pence. Americans Are Wary of Being Alone with the Opposite Sex," *New York Times*, July 1, 2017, www.nytimes.com/2017/07/01/upshot/members-of-the-opposite-sex-at-work-gender-study.html.

12. McKinsey & Company, Lean In, *Women in the Workplace 2016*, 23.

13. For a good account of this and other workplace issues, see Anne-Marie Slaughter, *Unfinished Business: Women, Men, Work, Family* (Toronto: Random House Canada, 2015).

14. One pioneering exception is in the male-dominated mining industry. As part of its participation in the White Ribbon Workplace Accreditation Program in Australia, Rio Tinto began offering a week of paid leave to staff experiencing domestic violence. At the time of writing, I'm part of an initiative supporting the extension of this policy to the United States and Canada.

15. Claire Suddath, "New Numbers Show the Gender Pay Gap Is Real," March 29, 2018. www.bloomberg.com/news/features/2018-03-29/the-gender-pay-gap-is-real-say-new-numbers-from-the-u-k .

16. Jon Henley, "'Equality won't happen by itself': How Iceland got tough on gender pay gap," *The Guardian*, February 20, 2018, www.theguardian.com/world/2018/feb/20/iceland-equal-pay-law-gender-gap-women-jobs-equality.

17. Chai R. Feldblum and Victoria A. Lipnic, *Select Task Force on the Study of Harassment in the Workplace*, Washington, D.C.: US Equal Employment Opportunity Commission, June 2016, 8–10.

18. Feldblum, *Select*, v.

19. This is based on an exercise by Jackson Katz. He in turn attributes the idea to the work of feminist anti-rape educators who would ask groups of women what they did to protect themselves.

5: The Dad Shift

1. Although my thinking about fatherhood started decades ago both as an active father and researcher, it developed significantly and greatly deepened while working with my friend and coauthor, Gary Barker, the international director of Promundo in Washington, D.C., where I am a senior fellow. This chapter owes a debt of gratitude to him and also to Nikki van der Gaag, Ruti Levtov, and Meg Greene with whom I coauthored *The State of the World's Fathers* in 2014–15. Indeed, thank you to all my colleagues at Promundo, MenCare, Save the Children, Rutgers, Sonke Gender Justice, and the MenEngage

Alliance for their work on that project. See R. Levtov, N. van der Gaag, M. Greene, M. Kaufman, and G. Barker, *State of the World's Fathers: A MenCare Advocacy Publication* (Washington, D.C.: Promundo, Rutgers, Save the Children, Sonke Gender Justice, and the MenEngage Alliance, 2015), sowf.men-care.org/wp-content /uploads/sites/4/2015/06/State-of-the-Worlds-Fathers-June2018 -web.pdf.

2. Anne Weisberg and Ellen Galinsky, *Family Matters: The Business Case for Investing in the Transition to Parenthood* (New York: Families and Work Institute, 2014), familiesandwork.org/downloads /Family-Matters.pdf.

3. Ellen Galinsky, Kerstin Aumann, and James T. Bond, *Times Are Changing: Gender and Generation at Work and at Home* (New York: Work and Families Institute, 2008, Revised 2011), 9.

4. B. Heilman, G. Cole, K. Matos, A. Hassink, R. Mincy, and G. Barker, *State of America's Fathers: A MenCare Advocacy Publication* (Washington, D.C.: Promundo-US, 2016), 37.

5. Shane Shifflett, Alissa Scheller, and Emily Peck, "The States with the Most Stay-at-Home Fathers," *Huffington Post*, accessed February 9, 2016, www.huffingtonpost.com/2015/05/13/stay-at-home -fathers_n_7261020.html.

6. Kimberley Fisher, Kimberley, Muriel Egerton, Jonathan I. Gershuny, and John P. Robinson, *Gender Convergence in the American Heritage Time Use Study (AHTUS)*, Social Indicators Research. DOI 10.1007/s11205-006-9017-y (2006).

7. Pew Research Center, "Moms and Dads, 1965–2011: Roles Converge, but Gaps Remain" (June 2015), www.pewresearch.org/fact -tank/2015/06/18/5-facts-about-todays-fathers/ft_moms-dads -family-roles-2. Please note that statistics used in this chapter come from many different studies. Because of difference in research methodologies (including the specific questions asked) there are differences in data—for example, in this stat on the drop of mothers' time doing housework and the previous stat for all women. The main point for my using these stats is (a) to show general trends, and (b) within a study, to show differences in fathers' and mothers' activities.

8. Fisher, *Gender Convergence.*
9. Suzanne M. Bianchi, John P. Robinson, and Melissa A. Milkie, *Changing Rhythms of American Family Life* (New York: Russell Sage Foundation Publications, Rose Series in Sociology, 2006).
10. K. Fisher, A. McCulloch, and J. Gershuny, *British fathers and children* (University of Essex: Institute for Social and Economic Research, working paper, 1999).
11. Adrienne Burgess "The Costs and Benefits of Active Fatherhood" (Fathers Direct/Fatherhood Institute, 2007), 7.
12. John Hoffman, "Father Factors: What Social Science Research Tells Us About Fathers and How to Work with Them" (Peterborough: Father Involvement Research Initiative, 2011).
13. Organization for Economic Cooperation and Development, 2017, stats.oecd.org/index.aspx?queryid=54757.
14. US and Canadian figures were for 2010, UK figures for 2006, Organisation for Economic Cooperation and Development totals for 2009–10. OECD, "Balancing paid work, unpaid work and leisure" (2014), www.oecd.org/gender/data/balancingpaidworkunpaidwork andleisure.htm.
15. Lee T. Gettler, "Direct Male Care and Hominin Evolution: Why Male-Child Interaction Is More Than a Nice Social Idea," *American Anthropologist,* vol. 112, Issue 1, 7; Sarah Blaffer Hrdy, *Mothers and Others: The Revolution Origins of Mutual Understanding* (Cambridge: Harvard University Press, 2009), chapter 1.
16. Hrdy, *Mothers and Others,* 169. Also see Paul Raeburn, *Do Fathers Matter? What Science Is Telling Us About the Parent We've Overlooked* (New York: Scientific America/Farrar, Straus and Giroux, 2014).
17. By contrast, leading up to giving birth, testosterone and estradiol levels in women increase, which gives a hint at the complexity of our endocrine systems and perhaps suggests that in parenting the average male/female hormonal mix converges at least to some extent. See Robin S. Edelstein, Britney M. Wardecker, William J. Chopik, Amy C. Moors, Emily L. Shipman, and Natalie J. Lin, "Prenatal Hormones in First-Time Expectant Parents: Longitudinal Changes

and Within-Couple Correlations," *American Journal of Human Biology*, online edition, 2014. And see Raeburn, *Do Fathers Matter?*

18. Gettler, "Direct Male Care...", 12.

19. Barry Hewlett, "Culture, History, and Sex: Anthropological Contributions to Conceptualizing Father Involvement," in *Fatherhood: Research, Interventions and Policies*, eds. H. Elizabeth Peters and Randal D. Day (Philadelphia: The Haworth Press, 2000), 63.

20. Erling Barth, Sari Pekkala Kerr, and Claudia Olivetti, "The Dynamics of Gender Earnings Differentials: Evidence from Establishment Data," National Bureau of Economic Research, Working Paper 23381, www.nber.org/papers/W23381, 2017; Claudia Goldin, Sari Pekkala Kerr, Claudia Olivetti, and Erling Barth, "The Expanding Gender Earnings Gap: Evidence from the LEHD-2000 Census," *American Economic Review*, 107(5): 110–14, doi .org/10.1257/aer.p20171065.

21. Scott Coltrane, "Father-child relationships and the status of women," 1988, in Hewlett 2000, 64.

22. See Burgess, "The Costs and Benefits...", 16 for references to a raft of studies.

23. Judith Yargawa and Jo Leonardi-Bee, "Male involvement and maternal health outcomes: systematic review and meta-analysis," *Journal of Epidemiological Community Health* (2015): 1–9, doi:10.1136 /jech-2014-204784.

24. Alfredo Pisacane, Grazia Isabella Continisio, Maria Aldinucci, Stefania D'Amora, and Paola Continisio, "A Controlled Trial of the Father's Role in Breastfeeding Promotion," *Pediatrics* (2005): 116; e494.

25. Among many sources, see R. D. Parke, "Fathers and families," in *Handbook of Parenting*, 2nd ed., Volume 3, ed. M. H. Bornstein, (Mahwah, NJ: Erlbaum Associates, 2002), 27–73.

26. Michael E. Lamb, "The Changing Faces of Fatherhood and Father-Child Relationships," in *Handbook of Family Theories*, eds. M. Fine and F. D. Fincham, (London: Routledge, 2013), 95–96; see also Michael E. Lamb, ed, *The Role of the Father in Child Development* (various editions).

27. Lamb, "The Changing Faces of Fatherhood...", 96.

28. Jo Jones and William D. Mosher, "Fathers' Involvement with Their Children: United States, 2006–2010," National Health Statistics Report No. 71, (December 20, 2013).

29. L. W. Hoffman and L. M. Youngblade, *Mothers at Work: Effects on Children's Well-being* (New York: Cambridge University Press, 1999).

30. Anna Sarkadi, Robert Kristiannsson, Frank Oberklaid, and Sven Bremberg, "Fathers' involvement and children's developmental outcomes: a systematic review of longitudinal studies," *Acta Pædiatrica* (September 2007).

31. Sarkadi, "Fathers' Involvement . . ."

32. Adrienne Burgess, "The Costs and Benefits of Active Fatherhood," Fathers Direct/Fatherhood Institute, 2007, 29. This report, available online (www.fatherhoodinstitute.org/uploads/publications /247.pdf), contains the largest bibliography of research in the field up to 2007. Also see the important work of Joseph Pleck over the years, including J. H. Pleck and B. P. Masciadrelli, "Paternal Involvement by US Residential Fathers: Levels, Sources and Consequences," in *The Role of the Father in Child Development* (4th ed.), ed. Michael E. Lamb (Hoboken, NJ: John Wiley & Sons, 2004).

33. C. E. Franz, D. C. McClelland, J. Weinberger, and C. Peterson, "Parenting Antecedents of Adult Adjustment: A Longitudinal Study," in *Parenting and Psychopathology*, ed. C. Perris, W. A. Arrindell, and M. Eisemann (New York: Wiley, 1994), and E. Flouri and A. Buchanan, "Life satisfaction in teenage boys: The moderating role of father involvement and bullying," *Aggressive Behavior* 28, (2002): 126–33.

34. Timothy S. Grail, "Custodial Mothers and Fathers and Their Child Support: 2009," US Census Bureau, US Department of Commerce (December 2011), 6, www.census.gov/prod/2011pubs/p60-240.pdf.

35. R. Levtov et al, *State of the World's Fathers (2015)*, 17. Also see Alyssa Croft, Toni Schmader, Katharina Block, and Andrew Baron, "The Second Shift Reflected in the Second Generation: Do Parents' Gender Roles at Home Predict Children's Aspirations?" (Vancouver: University of British Colombia, 2014), medicalxpress

.com/news/2014-05-dads-chores-bolster-daughters-aspirations
.html#nRlv.

36. Levtov et al, *State of the World's Fathers (2015)*, 42.

37. Thank you to Wessel van den Berg and my colleagues at Sonke Gender Justice for organizing my visit to Khayelitsha.

38. White Ribbon Campaign, "Give Love, Get Love. The Involved Father and Gender Equality Project" (Toronto: 2014), 33, 41, 55.

39. Kerry J. Daly, Lynda Ashbourne, and Jaime L. Brown, "A Reorientation of Worldview: Children's Influence on Fathers," *Journal of Family Issues*, 34 (10) 1401–1424 (2012): 1412–14.

40. D. J. Eggebeen and C. Knoester, "Does fatherhood matter for men?" *Journal of Marriage and Family*, vol. 63, no. 2 (May, 2001): 381–93.

41. L. Plantin, A. A. Olukoya, and P. Ny, "Positive Health Outcomes of Fathers' Involvement in Pregnancy and Childbirth Paternal Support: A Scope Study Literature Review," *Fathering* vol. 9, issue 1, (2001), 87–102.

42. R. A. Williams, "Masculinities and Fathering," *Community, Work & Family*, 12(1) (2008): 57–73.

43. Burgess, "The Costs and Benefits. . .", 22.

44. D. Lupton and L. Barclay, *Constructing Fatherhood: Discourses and Experiences* (London: Sage Publications, 1997), 15.

45. Eileen Patten and Kim Parker, "A Gender Reversal on Career Aspirations," Pew Research Center (April 19, 2001), www.pewsocial trends.org/2012/04/19/a-gender-reversal-on-career-aspirations.

46. Mary Gordon, *Roots of Empathy: Changing the World Child by Child* (Toronto: Thomas Allen, 2005 and 2012), www.rootsofempathy.org.

47. Heilman et al, *State of America's Fathers*, 85.

48. Julie Beck, "When Sex Ed Discusses Gender Inequality, Sex Gets Safer," *The Atlantic*, April 27, 2015, www.theatlantic.com/health /archive/2015/04/when-sex-ed-teaches-gender-inequality-sex-gets -safer/391460.

49. "State Policies on Sex Education in Schools," National Conference of State Legislatures, accessed May 8, 2016, www.ncsl.org/research /health/state-policies-on-sexeducation-in-schools.aspx.

50. Cynthia Dailard, "Sex Education: Politicians, Parents, Teachers and Teens," The Guttmacher Report on Public Policy 4, no. 1 (2001): 9–12.

51. Heilman et al, *State of America's Fathers*, 74.

52. Peter Moss, ed., "10th International Review of Leave Policies and Related Research 2014" (London: International Network on Leave Policies and Research, 2014).

53. Ankita Patnaik, "Making Leave Easier: Better Compensation and Daddy-Only Entitlement" (New York: Social Science Research Network, 2012) and P. Moss, ed., "10th International Review. . .".

54. We've done several reports at Promundo and MenCare on fatherhood. Some reports have been copublished by the United Nations Population Fund, Sonke Gender Justice, Save the Children, MenEngage, and Rutgers in the Netherlands. Among other things, these reports detail a broad range of critical government initiatives to transform fatherhood. The policy list in the text includes a few of many. See *State of the World's Fathers 2015*, *State of America's Fathers 2016*, *State of the World's Fathers 2017*, promundoglobal.org /resources.

55. Elly-Ann Johansson, "The Effect of Own and Spousal Parental Leave on Earnings" (Uppsala: The Institute for Labour Market Policy Evaluation, 2010).

56. Andreas Kotsadam and Henning Finseraas, "The State Intervenes in the Battle of the Sexes," *Social Science Research* 40 (2011): 1611–22.

6: Armistice Day

1. Jill Elaine Hasday, "Contest and Consent: A Legal History of Marital Rape," *California Law Review*, v. 88, issue 5 (October 2000), 1375–1505, scholarship.law.berkeley.edu/cgi/viewcontent .cgi?article=1484&context=californialawreview.

2. S. G. Smith, et. al., "The National Intimate Partner and Sexual Violence Survey (NISVS): 2010–2012 State Report" (Atlanta, GA: National Center for Injury Prevention and Control, Centers for Disease Control and Prevention, 2017).

3. Ibid.

4. European Union Agency for Fundamental Rights, "Violence Against Women, an EU-Wide Survey" (Vienna, 2014), 21–22.

5. Ibid, 71.

6. Ibid, 81.

7. Katie Sanders, "Steinem: More Women Killed by Partners Since 9/11 Than Deaths from Attacks, Ensuing Wars," *PunditFact*, October 7, 2014, www.politifact.com/punditfact/statements/2014/oct/07 /gloria-steinem/steinem-more-women-killed-partners-911-deaths-atta.

8. Deirdre Brennan, "Redefining an Isolated Incident," *Femicide Census, 2016*, 1q7dqy2unor827bqjls0c4rn-wpengine.netdna-ssl.com/wp -content/uploads/2017/01/The-Femicide-Census-Jan-2017.pdf.

9. United Nations, "International Day of Zero Tolerance for Female Genital Mutilation," February 6, 2018, www.un.org/en/events /femalegenitalmutilationday.

10. See titles like Marilyn French, *The War Against Women* (New York: Ballantine Books, 1992); World Health Organization, "Violence Against Women: A 'Global Health Problem of Epidemic Proportions'" (Geneva, June 20, 2013), www.who.int/mediacentre /news/releases/2013/violence_against_women_20130620/en; Conor Friedersdorf, "A Deadly Epidemic of Violence Against Women," *The Atlantic*, August 22, 2014.

11. Promundo, "International Men and Gender Equality Survey (IMAGES), promundoglobal.org/programs/international-men-and -gender-equality-survey-images.

12. Christopher J. Ferguson and Kevin M. Beaver, "Natural Born Killers: The Genetic Origins of Extreme Violence," in *Aggression and Violent Behavior*, vol 14, issue 15 (September–October 2009), 286–94.

13. Peggy Sanday, "The Sociocultural Context of Rape: A Cross-cultural Study," *The Journal of Social Issues* 37 (1981): 5–27; Peggy Sanday, *Female Power and Male Dominance* (New York: Cambridge University Press, 1981). Scott Coltrane's study of tribal societies again clearly showed the links between men's dominance and violence. Scott Coltrane, "The Micropolitics of Gender in Nonindustrial Societies," *Gender & Society* 6 (1992), 86–107.

14. Among the work I've done over the past twenty-five years has been training workshops for service providers and first responders in communities across North America and around the world. These are women who staff crisis lines and run shelters for women escaping abuse, they are female and male therapists, police officers, nurses, clergy, child-support workers, probation officers, and those working with men who have committed acts of violence. During these workshops and after other talks in communities, I've spoken to countless women who have told me about their escape from abusive relationships and also from some men who told me the excuses they once made. The accounts I've heard from them over the years is the basis for this composite character of Reg. My sincere thanks to all those who shared their insights and personal stories with me.

15. Connie Guberman and Margie Wolfe, eds., *No Safe Place* (Toronto: Women's Press, 1985), 14. Also see Michael Kaufman, "The Construction of Masculinity and the Triad of Men's Violence," in Michael Kaufman, ed., *Beyond Patriarchy: Essays by Men on Pleasure, Power, and Change* (Toronto: Oxford University Press, 1987) and at ecbiz194.inmotionhosting.com/~micha383/wp-content/uploads/2016/03/Kaufman-1987-The-Construction-of-Masculinity-and-the-Triad-of-Mens-Violence-in-Michael-Kaufman-ed.-Beyond-Patriarchy-Essays-by-Men-on-Pleasure-Power-and-....pdf

16. Samantha Allen, "Marital Rape is Semi-Legal in 8 States," *Daily Beast*, June 9, 2015, www.thedailybeast.com/marital-rape-is-semi-legal-in-8-states.

17. For programs working with coaches, see Mentors in Violence Prevention, www.mvpstrat.com; Futures Without Violence, "Coaching Boys Into Men," www.futureswithoutviolence.org/engaging-men/coaching-boys-into-men; and A Call to Men, www.acalltomen.org.

18. In 2015, 21.1 men per 100,000 US residents took their own lives, compared to 6 women: www.statista.com/statistics/187478/death-rate-from-suicide-in-the-us-by-gender-since-1950.

19. Joseph Strombreg, "The Microscopic Structures of Dried Human Tears," Smithsonion.com, November 19, 2013, www.smithsonian

mag.com/science-nature/the-microscopic-structures-of-dried-human-tears-180947766.

20. Coltrane, "Father-child relationships . . ."
21. See, for example, the wonderful account by Maia Szalavitz and Bruce D. Perry, *Born for Love: Why Empathy is Essential and Endangered* (New York: William Morrow, 2010).
22. Jessica Benjamin, *The Bonds of Love* (New York: Pantheon, 1985); Nancy Chodorow, *The Reproduction of Mothering* (Berkeley: University of California Press, 1978); Dorothy Dinnerstein, *The Mermaid and the Minotaur* (New York: Harper and Row, 1976).
23. B. Heilman, et al, *The Man Box*, 25, 28.
24. The first successful uprising against slavery in the Americas was the overthrow of slavery and French colonialism in Haiti between 1791 and 1804 led by Toussaint Louverture. Haiti became the second republic in the Americas.
25. Jackson Katz, "Violence Against Women—It's a Men's Issue," TedXxFiDiWomen, November 2012, www.ted.com/talks/jackson_katz_violence_against_women_it_s_a_men_s_issue.
26. For a critique of those who claim that violence by women against men is as extensive and harmful as violence by men against women, see the thoughtful article by Michael S. Kimmel, "'Gender symmetry' in domestic violence: A substantive and methodological research review," in *Violence Against Women, Special Issue: Women's Use of Violence in Intimate Relationships*, Part 1, 8 (11) (November 2002). Also available at the important website xyonline.net created by Michael Flood: xyonline.net/sites/xyonline.net/files/malevictims.pdf.
27. For a broader look at men's activism to end violence against women, see Michael A. Messner, Max A. Greenberg, and Tal Peretz, *Some Men: Feminist Allies and the Movement to End Violence Against Women* (New York: Oxford Univesity Press, 2015); Michael Flood, *Engaging Men and Boys in Violence Prevention* (Basingstoke, UK: Palgrave Macmillan, 2018).

7: Gender Equality and Beyond

1. Thanks to Fred Shapiro, editor of the *Yale Book of Quotations*, who

answered an online query about this: "The *Oxford English Dictionary* has as its earliest usage an article by Harriet Halter (titled 'Sex Roles and Social Change') in the journal *Acta Sociologica* (volume 14, page 10, 1971). I discovered another 1971 occurrence that may be earlier than Halter, namely a letter to the editor in the *Louisville Courier-Journal*, Mar. 9, 1971, by Gary Levenberger of Pleasure Ridge Park, Kentucky."

2. Michael Kimmel gives a very good presentation of this in *The Gendered Society*, 6th edition (New York: Oxford University Press, 2016).

3. The breakthrough challenge to this notion was in 1949 by Simone de Beauvoir, *The Second Sex*, translated and edited by H. M. Parshley (New York: Vintage Books, 1974), part 1.

4. Michael S. Kimmel, "Masculinity as Homophobia: Fear, Shame and Silence in the Construction of Gender Identity," in *Theorizing Masculinities*, ed. Harry Brod and Michael Kaufman (Thousand Oaks, CA: Sage Publications, 1994), 119–141.

5. Credit Suisse, *Global Wealth Databook 2017*. Accessed November 2017, www.credit-suisse.com/corporate/en/research/research-institute/publications.html. In Oxfam, "Reward Work, Not Wealth," Oxfam Briefing Paper (January 2018), 10.

6. Ronald Wright, *A Short History of Progress* (Toronto: Anansi, 2004 and New York: Carroll and Graf, 2005).

© Ali Kazimi

MICHAEL KAUFMAN, PhD, has spent almost four decades engaging men to support gender equality in efforts to transform the lives of both women and men. He's the co-founder of the White Ribbon Campaign, the largest international effort of men working to end violence against women. As an advisor and speaker, he has worked across North America and in fifty countries with the United Nations, governments, NGOs, and businesses. He grew up in Ohio and North Carolina and lives in Toronto, Canada. He is a senior fellow with Promundo, based in Washington, D.C. Kaufman is the author or editor of eight books.